BLS WORKING PAPERS

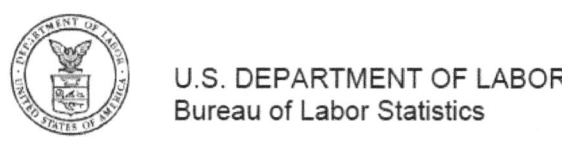

U.S. DEPARTMENT OF LABOR
Bureau of Labor Statistics

OFFICE OF PRICES AND LIVING
CONDITIONS

Imputation and Price Indexes: Theory and Evidence
from the International Price Program

Robert C. Feenstra, University of California, Davis
Erwin W. Diewert, University of British Columbia

Working Paper 335
January 2001

The views expressed are those of the authors and do not necessarily reflect the policies of the U.S. Bureau of Labor Statistics or the views of other staff members.   This paper was part of the U.S. Bureau of Labor Statistics Conference on *Issues in Measuring Price Change and Consumption* in Washington, DC, June 2000.

Imputation and Price Indexes:

Theory and Evidence from the International Price Program[1]

by

Robert C. Feenstra,
University of California, Davis, and NBER

and

Erwin W. Diewert,
University of British Columbia and NBER

Revised, June 2000

---

[1] The authors thank William Alterman, Paul Armknecht, Marvin Kasper and Fenella Maitland-Smith for helpful discussions and correspondence.

1. Introduction

Published price indexes are nearly always constructed from individual prices collected by some sampling framework, were the samples are chosen, in part, to minimize the time and expense involved in collecting the prices. In particular, the time spent by reporting firms or consumers is quite rightly treated as precious. It is inevitable that questionnaires sent out in repeated months will sometimes not be returned. For example, about *one-quarter* of the individual items tracked under the International Price Program (IPP) of the Bureau of Labor Statistics (BLS) *do not* report a price in any given month, though of these, about 60% eventually supply a price quote for that month or a later month. This means that there is a substantial number of individual prices that are *missing* at the time the monthly index must be constructed and published. For this reason, the IPP program *imputes* the missing prices, and we expect that this practice is followed by many other statistical agencies in the U.S. and abroad. Despite this common practice, there has been practically no theoretical or empirical work examining the consequences of different imputation methods (a notable exception is Armknecht and Maitland-Smith, 1999). The goal of this paper is to begin to fill this theoretical gap, and also demonstrate the consequences of different imputation methods using recent data from the IPP.

Price quotations could be missing for a number of reasons, including the following ones:

- Observations could be missing due to random or erratic reporting on the part of respondents;
- Observations could be missing due to strong seasonality in the pattern of production;
- Observations could be missing due to technological progress or changing market conditions; i.e., new models or varieties replace the commodities that were in the initial sampling frame.

Obviously, seasonal commodities that are sold in the marketplace for only certain months of the year will give rise to missing observations. Similarly, the replacement of an "old" commodity by a "new" one will also lead to missing observations (for the old commodities).

An appropriate treatment of seasonal commodities that are available only in certain months of the year leads to complexities that we will not address here.[2] Also, we will not deal with the disappearing goods problem in this draft. Thus, we concentrate on the first reason for missing price quotations: random or erratic reporting. With the problem of missing observations narrowed down to the first reason, the situation is similar to that used in the *stochastic approach to index number theory.*[3]

Before we develop the theory, it will be useful to frame the problem a bit more. The first thing we have to decide is: what index are we trying to construct? We assume that *the goal is to construct a fixed base Laspeyres price index.* As mentioned above, we ignore the seasonality and new goods problems for now. Thus assume that we have a sample of base period 0 prices, p_n^0, that pertain to some class of commodities for say January of the base year. We follow that

---

[2] For an introduction to these index number complexities and references to the literature, see Alterman, Diewert and Feenstra (1999) and Diewert (1998) (1999).

[3] Recent references to the literature on the stochastic approach to index number theory include Bryan and Cecchetti (1993) (1994), Ceccheti (1997), Clements and Izan (1987), Diewert (1995) (1997), Selvanathan and Rao (1994) and Wynne (1997) (1999).

sample of commodity prices up to the current period t and these period t prices are p_n^t for n = 1,2,...,N. We also have some base period sample weights, w_n^0, for n = 1,2,...,N. Now assume that in period t > 0, that some price quotes are missing for whatever reason. Denote the set of commodity indexes for which we have price information in period t by S(t). Then a possible candidate for estimating the true fixed base Laspeyres index for period t is the following index:

$$(1) \qquad P_L(0,t) \equiv \sum_{n \in S(t)} w_n^0 \, (p_n^t/p_n^0) \, / \sum_{n \in S(t)} w_n^0 \; ;$$

i.e., we take the summation over quotes n in period t for which we have real information, and we rescale the weights w_n^0 so that they sum to 1. This avoids the problem of imputing prices for missing observations and it appears that this is the end of the story.

But is this the end of the story? The answer is *yes* if all price relatives have the same mean whether they are in the current sample or not. The answer is *no* if the pattern of price movements for commodities that are always in the sample is different from the pattern of price changes for commodities that do not have reported price quotes for every period. In our empirical work, we find that the answer is no rather than yes. Thus if price relatives in the current sample have a different mean than price relatives that are not in the current sample, as commodities rotate in and out of the sample, we would find a certain amount of spurious price "bouncing" in our estimated long term Laspeyres index.

In an effort to minimize this price bouncing behavior, one approach would be to use the following *modified Laspeyres index* for period t:

$$(2) \qquad P_{ML}(0,t) \equiv \sum_{n \in S(t) \cap S(t-1)} w_n^0 \, (p_n^t/p_n^0) \, / \sum_{n \in S(t) \cap S(t-1)} w_n^0 \; ;$$

i.e., the summation is now taken over the *intersection* of the quotes or commodities that are present in the marketplace during *both* periods t-1 and t. This new index will ensure that like is being compared with like when we go from period t-1 to period t but in order to eliminate the bouncing phenomenon entirely over the entire sample period, we would have to restrict the summation in (2) to commodities that have reported price quotes in *every* period. This would drastically reduce the effective sample size. Even comparing (1) with (2), we see that (1) is the most accurate long term index for period t that makes full use of the available information. Put another way, the modified Laspeyres formula (2) throws away useful information.

The actual method used by the IPP differs slightly from (2), and instead considers the *ratio* of these long term Laspeyres indexes:

$$(3) \qquad P_R(t-1,t) \equiv [\sum_{n \in S(t) \cap S(t-1)} w_n^0 \, (p_n^t/p_n^0) \,] / [\sum_{n \in S(t) \cap S(t-1)} w_n^0 \, (p_n^{t-1}/p_n^0)]$$

i.e., the summation in the numerator and denominator is now taken over the *intersection* of the quotes or commodities that are present in the marketplace during *both* periods t-1 and t. Given this short term index, the long term index is then obtained by the cumulative formula,

$$(4) \qquad P_R(0,t) \equiv P_R(0,t-1) \, P_R(t-1,t), \text{ with } P_R(0,0) \equiv 1.$$

Summing up, we have introduced three methods of constructing indexes when the set of commodities is changing over time: the fixed base Laspeyres index in (1), which uses all the information available; the *modified* Laspeyres index in (2), which uses the same set of commodities in periods t-1 and t; and the *Laspeyres-ratio* method in (3) and (4), which first constructs the short term index, and then cumulates it to obtain the long term index. It is immediate that if the set of commodities is equal over time, then these three methods are equivalent, but otherwise they are not. The question then arises as to which index method would best approximate the (unobserved) fixed base Laspeyres index that does not suffer from the missing prices.

The above descriptive material should give the reader an indication of the problems that we are attempting to address. In section 2 below, we introduce a somewhat artificial model where some commodities have price quotes for every period, some commodities have price quotes available for only odd numbered periods and some commodities have price quotes available for only even numbered periods. In section 3, we derive the long term fixed base Laspeyres index that corresponds to (1) above (in the context of our simple model) and show that it is consistent with a simple imputation procedure. In section 4, we consider the *actual* imputation method used by the Bureau of Labor Statistics (BLS), and other agencies, which is most similar to the formulas (3)-(4), but extends these by *imputing* some of the "missing" prices. In section 5, we allow revisions to indexes and consider imputation procedures based on interpolation methods that seems superior to those considered in sections 3 and 4. Following this, in sections 6-9 the various imputation methods are evaluated using data from the International Prices Program (IPP) of the BLS.

2. A Simple Model

We assume that there are three classes of commodities under consideration:

- Commodities that have price quotes available in every period. We assume that there are N such commodities (or reporting units) and the price and quantity vectors for these always available commodities are $p^t \equiv (p_1^t,...,p_N^t)$ for periods $t = 0,1,2,...,T$. There is also information available on a base period quantity vector, $q^0 \equiv (q_1^0,...,q_N^0)$.

- Commodities that report price quotes only for odd numbered periods (in addition to the base period 0). We assume that there are J such commodities (or reporting units) and the price vectors for these commodities are $u^t \equiv (u_1^t,...,u_J^t)$ for $t = 0,1,2,...,T$. However, we only are able to observe these price vectors for periods 0,1,3,5,.... We also assume that we can observe the period 0 quantity vector for these commodities, $x^0 \equiv (x_1^0,...,x_J^0)$.

- Commodities that report price quotes only for even numbered periods. We assume that there are K such commodities (or reporting units) and the price vectors for these commodities are $v^t \equiv (v_1^t,...,v_K^t)$ for $t = 0,1,2,...,T$. However, we only are able to observe these price vectors for periods 0,2,4,.... We also assume that we can observe the period 0 quantity vector for these commodities, $y^0 \equiv (y_1^0,...,y_K^0)$.

Thus our *visible* data array can be written in tabular form as follows:

Period	Prices			Quantities		
0	p^0	u^0	v^0	q^0	x^0	y^0
1	p^1	u^1		—	—	—
2	p^2		$\overline{v^2}$	—	—	—
3	p^3	$\overline{u^3}$		—	—	—
4	p^4	—	$\overline{v^4}$	—	—	—
...		...			...	

We assume that our goal is to construct the sequence of *fixed base Laspeyres price indexes* $\overline{P}_L(0,t)$ defined as follows:

$$(5) \qquad \overline{P}_L(0,t) \equiv [p^t \bullet q^0 + u^t \bullet x^0 + v^t \bullet y^0] / [p^0 \bullet q^0 + u^0 \bullet x^0 + v^0 \bullet y^0] ; \qquad t = 0,1,2,...,T$$

where $p^t \bullet q^0 \equiv \sum_{n=1}^{N} p_n^t q_n^0$ denotes the inner product between the vectors p^t and q^0, etc. Of course, our problem is that we do not have all of the price information available to calculate the sequence of fixed base Laspeyres indexes defined by (5).

It will be useful to define the sequence of *fixed base Laspeyres price indexes, $P_\alpha(0,t)$, over the set of always available commodities* as follows:

$$
\begin{aligned}
(6) \qquad P_\alpha(0,t) &\equiv p^t \bullet q^0 / p^0 \bullet q^0 & t = 1,2,....,T \\
&= \sum_{n=1}^{N} p_n^t q_n^0 / p^0 \bullet q^0 \\
&= \sum_{n=1}^{N} [p_n^t / p_n^0] p_n^0 q_n^0 / p^0 \bullet q^0 \\
&= \sum_{n=1}^{N} w_n^0 [p_n^t / p_n^0]
\end{aligned}
$$

where the base period expenditure share of commodity n compared to the total base period expenditures of always reported commodities is w_n^0 defined by

$$(7) \qquad w_n^0 \equiv p_n^0 q_n^0 / p^0 \bullet q^0 ; \qquad\qquad n = 1,2,...,N.$$

Thus from the last line of equations (6), we see that $P_\alpha(0,t)$ is a base period share weighted average of the period t long term price relatives, p_n^t / p_n^0. If we take the stochastic approach to index number theory, we could assume that each of these price relatives has the same mean and then the Laspeyres index $P_\alpha(0,t)$ would be a good estimator for this unknown mean.

In a similar fashion, it is useful to define the sequence of *fixed base Laspeyres price indexes, $P_\beta(0,t)$, over the set of commodities, reported only in odd periods,* as follows:

$$
\begin{aligned}
(8) \qquad P_\beta(0,t) &\equiv u^t \bullet x^0 / u^0 \bullet x^0 & t = 1,2,....,T \\
&= \sum_{j=1}^{J} u_j^t x_j^0 / u^0 \bullet x^0 \\
&= \sum_{j=1}^{J} [u_j^t / u_j^0] u_j^0 x_j^0 / u^0 \bullet x^0 \\
&= \sum_{j=1}^{J} w_j^0 [u_j^t / u_j^0]
\end{aligned}
$$

where the base period expenditure share of commodity j compared to the total base period expenditures of commodities available only in odd periods is w_j^0 defined by

$$(9) \qquad w_j^0 \equiv u_j^0 \, x_j^0 \,/\, u^0 \bullet x^0 \,; \qquad\qquad\qquad\qquad j = 1,2,\ldots,J.$$

Again, we see that $P_\beta(0,t)$ is a base period share weighted average of the period t long term price relatives, $u_j^t \,/\, u_j^0$. If we take the stochastic approach to index number theory, we can again assume that each of these price relatives has the same mean and then the Laspeyres index $P_\beta(0,t)$ is a good estimator for this unknown mean. Note that we have defined $P_\beta(0,t)$ for all periods t even though we can observe $P_\beta(0,t)$ only for odd numbered periods. Thus the situation is different than it was for the $P_\alpha(0,t)$ term Laspeyres indexes, which were observable for every period.

Finally, it is useful to define the sequence of *fixed base Laspeyres price indexes*, $P_\gamma(0,t)$, *over the set of commodities reported only in even periods* as follows:

$$(10) \qquad P_\gamma(0,t) \equiv v^t \bullet y^0 \,/\, v^0 \bullet y^0 \qquad\qquad\qquad t = 1,2,\ldots,T$$
$$= \sum_{k=1}^K v_k^t \, y_k^0 \,/\, v^0 \bullet y^0$$
$$= \sum_{k=1}^K [v_k^t \,/\, v_k^0] \, v_k^0 \, y_k^0 \,/\, v^0 \bullet y^0$$
$$= \sum_{k=1}^K w_k^0 \, [v_k^t \,/\, v_k^0]$$

where the base period expenditure share of commodity k compared to the total base period expenditures of commodities available only in even periods is w_k^0 defined by

$$(11) \qquad w_k^0 \equiv v_k^0 \, y_k^0 \,/\, v^0 \bullet y^0 \,; \qquad\qquad\qquad\qquad k = 1,2,\ldots,K.$$

Again, we see that $P_\gamma(0,t)$ is a base period share weighted average of the period t long term price relatives, $v_k^t \,/\, v_k^0$. If we again take the stochastic approach to index number theory, we can assume that each of these price relatives has the same mean and then the Laspeyres index $P_\gamma(0,t)$ is a good estimator for this unknown mean. Note that we have defined $P_\gamma(0,t)$ for all periods t even though we can observe $P_\gamma(0,t)$ only for even numbered periods. It is this *lack of observability* for $P_\beta(0,t)$ and $P_\gamma(0,t)$ for even and odd periods that causes the problems that we attempt to address in the remainder of this paper.

We can use the above definitions to rewrite the true long term Laspeyres price index for period t, defined by (5) above, as follows:

$$(12) \;\; \overline{P}_L(0,t) \equiv [p^t \bullet q^0 + u^t \bullet x^0 + v^t \bullet y^0] \,/\, [p^0 \bullet q^0 + u^0 \bullet x^0 + v^0 \bullet y^0]\,; \qquad t = 0,1,2,\ldots,T$$
$$= \{p^0 \bullet q^0 [p^t \bullet q^0 /\, p^0 \bullet q^0] + u^0 \bullet x^0 \, [u^t \bullet x^0 /\, u^0 \bullet x^0] + v^0 \bullet y^0 \, [v^t \bullet y^0 / v^0 \bullet y^0]\} / [p^0 \bullet q^0 + u^0 \bullet x^0 + v^0 \bullet y^0] =$$
$$\{p^0 \bullet q^0 \, [P_\alpha(0,t)] + u^0 \bullet x^0 \, [P_\beta(0,t)] + v^0 \bullet y^0 \, [P_\gamma(0,t)]\} \,/\, [p^0 \bullet q^0 + u^0 \bullet x^0 + v^0 \bullet y^0]$$
$$= w_\alpha \, [P_\alpha(0,t)] + w_\beta \, [P_\beta(0,t)] + w_\gamma \, [P_\gamma(0,t)]$$

where the base period expenditure share of *always reported commodities* is

(13) $w_\alpha \equiv p^0 \bullet q^0 / [p^0 \bullet q^0 + u^0 \bullet x^0 + v^0 \bullet y^0]$;

and the base period expenditure share of commodities that are reported only in *odd periods* is

(14) $w_\beta \equiv u^0 \bullet x^0 / [p^0 \bullet q^0 + u^0 \bullet x^0 + v^0 \bullet y^0]$;

and the base period expenditure share of commodities that are reported only in *even periods* is

(15) $w_\gamma \equiv v^0 \bullet y^0 / [p^0 \bullet q^0 + u^0 \bullet x^0 + v^0 \bullet y^0]$.

Given the above definitions, we can now frame our imputation problem as follows. We want to estimate the true long term Laspeyres index defined by (12) above, but we can only observe two of the three components that make up this index in any given time period. Our imputation problem can be summarized by the following table:

Table 1: The Long Term True Laspeyres Index and its Observable Components

Period	True index	Observable components
1	$w_\alpha P_\alpha(0,1) + w_\beta P_\beta(0,1) + w_\gamma P_\gamma(0,1)$	$P_\alpha(0,1)$, $P_\beta(0,1)$, ___
2	$w_\alpha P_\alpha(0,2) + w_\beta P_\beta(0,2) + w_\gamma P_\gamma(0,2)$	$P_\alpha(0,2)$, ___ , $P_\gamma(0,2)$
3	$w_\alpha P_\alpha(0,3) + w_\beta P_\beta(0,3) + w_\gamma P_\gamma(0,3)$	$P_\alpha(0,3)$, $P_\beta(0,3)$, ___
4	$w_\alpha P_\alpha(0,4) + w_\beta P_\beta(0,4) + w_\gamma P_\gamma(0,4)$	$P_\alpha(0,4)$, ___ , $P_\gamma(0,4)$
5	$w_\alpha P_\alpha(0,5) + w_\beta P_\beta(0,5) + w_\gamma P_\gamma(0,5)$	$P_\alpha(0,5)$, $P_\beta(0,5)$, ___
…	…	…

In the above table, it is assumed that we know the base period expenditure shares, w_α, w_β and w_γ defined by (13) to (15) above.

We can first check the index methods mentioned in the introduction. It is readily seen that the Laspeyres-ratio defined by (3) above yields the following index, using our new notation:

(16) $P_R(t-1,t) = P_\alpha(0,t) / P_\alpha(0,t-1)$,   t = 1,2,…,T.

so that either the cumulated index or the modified Laspeyres are simply,

(17) $P_R(0,t) = P_{ML}(0,t) = P_\alpha(0,t)$.   t = 1,2,…,T.

In other words, the long term modified Laspeyres and the Laspeyres-ratio cumulated indexes are equivalent in this model, and simply yield the price index constructed over the *always available* commodities. These indexes are fine provided that the movements of intermittently available prices is the same as the movements in the always available prices. Unfortunately, our IPP data will not support this assumption; i.e., intermittently available prices seem to have a slightly different long term trend compared to always available prices.[4]

In the following three sections, we consider alternative imputation schemes to "fill in" some of the missing prices.

3. A Long Term Cell Mean Method of Imputation

Our first method imputes the missing long term price relatives by taking the (base period weighted) *mean* of the long term price relatives that are reported. We call this the *long term cell mean method of imputation*.

If t is odd, then the weighted mean of the long term price relatives that are available in period t is:

$$(18) \quad P_\gamma^*(0,t) \equiv [w_\alpha P_\alpha(0,t) + w_\beta P_\beta(0,t)]/(w_\alpha + w_\beta) , \qquad t = 1,3,5,....$$

Hence if t is odd, we estimate the imputed prices for the missing commodities as,

$$(19) \quad v_k^{t*} \equiv v_k^0 P_\gamma^*(0,t) \qquad \text{for } k = 1,2,...,K$$

Since all these imputed prices are growing at the same rate, when they are aggregated using the weights w_k^0, we obtain the long term Laspeyres index defined by (18). We therefore estimate the long term Laspeyres index by the following index, which replaces the true $P_\gamma(0,t)$ by $P_\gamma^*(0,t)$:

$$(20) \quad P^*(0,t) \equiv w_\alpha P_\alpha(0,t) + w_\beta P_\beta(0,t) + w_\gamma [P_\gamma^*(0,t)]$$
$$= w_\alpha P_\alpha(0,t) + w_\beta P_\beta(0,t) + w_\gamma[w_\alpha P_\alpha(0,t) + w_\beta P_\beta(0,t)]/ (w_\alpha + w_\beta), \text{ using (18)}$$
$$= (w_\alpha + w_\beta + w_\gamma)\{[w_\alpha P_\alpha(0,t) + w_\beta P_\beta(0,t)]/ (w_\alpha + w_\beta)\}$$
$$= [w_\alpha P_\alpha(0,t) + w_\beta P_\beta(0,t)]/ (w_\alpha + w_\beta), \text{ since } (w_\alpha + w_\beta + w_\gamma) =1,$$
$$= P_L(0,t), \text{ from (1).}$$

Thus, the long term Laspeyres index that uses the imputed price defined by (18)-(19) turns out to equal the long term Laspeyres index defined in (1), that just uses all the available price quotes. In other words, adding imputed prices *based on their long term cell mean imputation* is exactly the same as *not using imputed prices* in the long term index.

On reflection, this result is not that surprising. By *not using* any imputed prices in (1), the index weights are simply apportioned over all the commodities whose prices are available. Armknecht and Maitland-Smith (1999, p. 6) refer to this as "implicit" imputation. In contrast, "explicit" imputation occurs when values for the missing prices are actually imputed, and explicitly used in the index calculation. As Armknecht and Maitland-Smith note, if the imputed values are set

[4] Put another way, the index method defined by (17) makes no use of the intermittently available information, so it is unlikely that this method is statistically efficient.

equal to the price index for the group of goods in question (where initially this price index is computed without any imputed values), then when we re-compute the price index taking into account these imputed values, its value will not change at all. In this sense, "implicit" is equivalent to "explicit" imputation when the group price index is used to impute missing values, and that is what we have confirmed.

Similarly, for even periods t, the imputed prices are:

$$(21) \quad u_j^{t*} \equiv u_j^0 \, P_\beta^*(0,t) \qquad\qquad \text{for } j = 1,2,\ldots,J,$$

where,

$$(22) \quad P_\beta^*(0,t) \equiv [w_\alpha \, P_\alpha(0,t) + w_\gamma \, P_\gamma(0,t)]/(w_\alpha + w_\gamma) . \qquad t = 2,4,6,\ldots$$

Again, we estimate the long term Laspeyres index by replacing the true $P_\beta(0,t)$ with its imputed value $P_\beta^*(0,t)$:

$$
\begin{aligned}
(23) \quad P^*(0,t) &\equiv w_\alpha \, P_\alpha(0,t) + w_\beta \, [P_\beta^*(0,t)] + w_\gamma \, P_\gamma(0,t) \\
&= w_\alpha \, P_\alpha(0,t) + w_\beta \, [w_\alpha P_\alpha(0,t) + w_\gamma P_\gamma(0,t)]/(w_\alpha + w_\gamma) + w_\gamma \, P_\gamma(0,t), \text{ using (22)} \\
&= (w_\alpha + w_\beta + w_\gamma)\{[w_\alpha P_\alpha(0,t) + w_\gamma \, P_\gamma(0,t)]/(w_\alpha + w_\gamma)\} \\
&= [w_\alpha P_\alpha(0,t) + w_\gamma P_\gamma(0,t)]/(w_\alpha + w_\gamma), \text{ since } (w_\alpha + w_\beta + w_\gamma) = 1, \\
&= P_L(0,t), \quad \text{from (1)}.
\end{aligned}
$$

This is the same result as in (20), that imputing prices *based on their long term cell mean imputation* is exactly the same as *not using imputed prices* in the long term index.

The imputed indexes $P^*(0,t)$ can be compared to the true (but unobservable) sequence of Laspeyres indexes $\overline{P}_L(0,t)$ defined by (12) as follows:

Table 2: Long Term Cell Mean Imputed Laspeyres Indexes

Period	True index $\overline{P}_L(0,t)$	Imputed Index $P^*(0,t)$
1	$w_\alpha \, P_\alpha(0,1) + w_\beta \, P_\beta(0,1) + w_\gamma \, P_\gamma(0,1)$	$[w_\alpha \, P_\alpha(0,1) + w_\beta \, P_\beta(0,1)]/(w_\alpha + w_\beta)$
2	$w_\alpha \, P_\alpha(0,2) + w_\beta \, P_\beta(0,2) + w_\gamma \, P_\gamma(0,2)$	$[w_\alpha \, P_\alpha(0,2) + w_\gamma \, P_\gamma(0,2)]/(w_\alpha + w_\gamma)$
3	$w_\alpha \, P_\alpha(0,3) + w_\beta \, P_\beta(0,3) + w_\gamma \, P_\gamma(0,3)$	$[w_\alpha \, P_\alpha(0,3) + w_\beta \, P_\beta(0,3)]/(w_\alpha + w_\beta)$
4	$w_\alpha \, P_\alpha(0,4) + w_\beta \, P_\beta(0,4) + w_\gamma \, P_\gamma(0,4)$	$[w_\alpha \, P_\alpha(0,4) + w_\gamma \, P_\gamma(0,4)]/(w_\alpha + w_\gamma)$
5	$w_\alpha \, P_\alpha(0,5) + w_\beta \, P_\beta(0,5) + w_\gamma \, P_\gamma(0,5)$	$[w_\alpha \, P_\alpha(0,5) + w_\beta \, P_\beta(0,5)]/(w_\alpha + w_\beta)$
…	…	…

It can be seen that the long term cell mean method of imputation does better than the methods presented in the earlier section in the sense that it *makes use of all of the available information*. However, if the even period and odd period price quotes have different trends in them, it can be seen that the imputed indexes will have a tendency to "bounce" from period to period.[5] Moreover, even if the β and γ trends are *identical* (but not equal to the α trend), then it can be seen that the imputed index $P^*(0,t)$ gives *too small a weight* to the β and γ trends.

To formalize the intuition that the imputed index will tend to "bounce", let us define the period-to-period change in the index $P^*(0,t)$, measured *relative to* the always available commodities $P_\alpha(0,t)$, as:

(24) $\Delta^*(t-1,t) \equiv [P^*(0,t)/ P_\alpha(0,t) - P^*(0,t-1)/ P_\alpha(0,t-1)]$.

Then the following result is proved in the Appendix:

Proposition 1

Assume that $w_\beta = w_\gamma > 0$. If,

(25) $P_\beta(0,t) \geq P_\alpha(0,t) \geq P_\gamma(0,t)$ for all t=1,...,T,

or the reverse inequalities hold for all t, then:

(a) $\Delta^*(t-1,t)\Delta^*(t-2,t-1) \leq 0$;

(b) $|\Delta^*(t-2,t)| \leq \max \{ |\Delta^*(t-2,t-1)| , |\Delta^*(t-1,t)| \}$.

To interpret these results, part (a) says that the index $P^*(0,t)$, measured relative to $P_\alpha(0,t)$, moves in *opposite directions* between periods t-2 to t-1, and t-1 to t. This is the "bouncing" phenomena that we described above, and applies whenever (25) (or the reverse inequalities) hold. We interpret part (a) as saying there is *negative autocorrelation* in the index $P^*(0,t)$. An implication of this is that *absolute value of the two period* difference, as measured by $|\Delta^*(t-2,t)|$, is *less than the highest of the absolute value of the one period changes*, as stated in part (b). Thus, the bouncing behavior is "smoothed out" when we compare just even periods, or just odd periods.

We now turn to a second imputation method, to see if it can reduce some of the erratic movement in the price index.

4. A Short Term Cell Mean Method of Imputation.

The method of imputation that we propose in the present section imputes the missing price quotes for the current period using the movements in the *short term price relatives* for quotes that are available for both the current period and the preceding period. We call this the *short term cell mean method of imputation,* and it is similar to that actually used by the IPP.[6]

---

[5] If the lack of reporting is due to seasonality, then it is quite likely that the even period prices have a different trend than the odd period prices.

[6] The IPP program imputes prices exactly as in (28) and (30) below, but P_α is the Laspeyres-ratio defined over the intersection of price quotes available this period and price quotes *or imputed prices* available last period. In

For consecutive periods t-1 and t, the short term Laspeyres-ratio index that uses only information on price quotes that are available in both periods is:

(26) $P_\alpha(t-1,t) \equiv [\sum_{n=1}^{N} w_n^0 (p_n^t/p_n^0)]/[\sum_{n=1}^{N} w_n^0 (p_n^{t-1}/p_n^0)]$ t = 2,3,4,...,T
          $= P_\alpha(0,t)/ P_\alpha(0,t-1)$, using (6).

With the help of (26), we are now ready to impute prices for our missing long term price relatives.

In period 1, the prices v_k^1 are missing. However, we have two sets of short term price relatives that are observable in period 1, namely the price relatives p_n^1/p_n^0 that are in the Laspeyres index $P_\alpha(0,1)$ defined by (6) and the price relatives u_j^1/u_j^0 that are in the Laspeyres index $P_\beta(0,1)$ defined by (8). Thus in this case, our short run cell mean imputation for γ_1 is

(27) $v_k^{1**} \equiv v_k^0 [w_\alpha P_\alpha(0,1) + w_\beta P_\beta(0,1)]/ (w_\alpha + w_\beta)$ k=1,...,K.

Aggregating the imputed prices v_k^{1**} using the weights w_k^0, we just obtain the index $P_\gamma*(0,1)$ defined in (18), and (19)-(20) follow much the same for period 1.

In period 2, the prices u_j^2 are missing. We impute these by escalating their previous period prices u_j^1, using the index $P_\alpha(1,2)$. Thus, for t even our estimator for the missing prices is:

(28) $u_j^{t**} \equiv u_j^{t-1} P_\alpha(t-1,t)$;   t = 2,4,6,....

Aggregating these using the weights w_j^0, we obtain the imputed index,

(29) $P_\beta**(0,t) \equiv P_\beta(0,t-1) P_\alpha(t-1,t)$;   t = 2,4,6,....

In period 3, the prices v_k^3 are missing. We impute these by escalating their previous period prices v_k^3, using the index $P_\alpha(2,3)$. In general, for t odd our estimator for the missing prices is:

(30) $v_k^{t**} \equiv v_k^{t-1} P_\alpha(t-1,t)$;   t = 3,5,7,....

Aggregating these using the weights w_k^0, we obtain the imputed index,

(31) $P_\gamma**(0,t) \equiv P_\gamma(0,t-1) P_\alpha(t-1,t)$;   t = 3,5,7,....

---

contrast, we are defining P_α over just the price quotes available both periods. Another difference between IPP procedures and what we discuss in this section is that the IPP constructs the long term index using the cumulating procedure like (3)-(4), whereas we construct it as in (32) and (33).

Hence if t is odd, we estimate the true long term Laspeyres index by the following index, which replaces the true $P_\gamma(0,t)$ by $P_\gamma^{**}(0,t)$:

(32) $P^{**}(0,t) \equiv w_\alpha P_\alpha(0,t) + w_\beta P_\beta(0,t) + w_\gamma[P_\gamma^{**}(0,t)]$, $t = 1,3,5,...$

         $= [w_\alpha + w_\gamma P_\gamma(0,t-1)/P_\alpha(0,t-1)]P_\alpha(0,t) + w_\beta P_\beta(0,t)$,   using (26) and (31).

Similarly, if t is even, we estimate the true long term Laspeyres index by the following index, which replaces the true $P_\beta(0,t)$ by $P_\beta^{**}(0,t)$:

(33) $P^{**}(0,t) \equiv w_\alpha P_\alpha(0,t) + w_\beta [P_\beta^{**}(0,t)] + w_\gamma P_\gamma(0,t)$, $t = 2,4,6,...$

         $= [w_\alpha + w_\beta P_\beta(0,t-1)/P_\alpha(0,t-1)]P_\alpha(0,t) + w_\gamma P_\gamma(0,t)$,   using (26) and (29)

The imputed indexes $P^{**}(0,t)$ can be compared to the true (but unobservable) sequence of Laspeyres indexes $\overline{P}_L(0,t)$ defined by (12) as follows:

Table 3: Short Term Cell Mean Imputed Laspeyres Indexes

Period	True index $\overline{P}_L(0,t)$	Imputed Index $P^{**}(0,t)$
1	$w_\alpha P_\alpha(0,1) + w_\beta P_\beta(0,1) + w_\gamma P_\gamma(0,1)$	$[w_\alpha P_\alpha(0,1) + w_\beta P_\beta(0,1)]/ (w_\alpha + w_\beta)$
2	$w_\alpha P_\alpha(0,2) + w_\beta P_\beta(0,2) + w_\gamma P_\gamma(0,2)$	$[w_\alpha + w_\beta P_\beta(0,1)/P_\alpha(0,1)]P_\alpha(0,2) + w_\gamma P_\gamma(0,2)$
3	$w_\alpha P_\alpha(0,3) + w_\beta P_\beta(0,3) + w_\gamma P_\gamma(0,3)$	$[w_\alpha + w_\gamma P_\gamma(0,2)/P_\alpha(0,2)]P_\alpha(0,3) + w_\beta P_\beta(0,3)$
4	$w_\alpha P_\alpha(0,4) + w_\beta P_\beta(0,4) + w_\gamma P_\gamma(0,4)$	$[w_\alpha + w_\beta P_\beta(0,3)/P_\alpha(0,3)]P_\alpha(0,4) + w_\gamma P_\gamma(0,4)$
5	$w_\alpha P_\alpha(0,5) + w_\beta P_\beta(0,5) + w_\gamma P_\gamma(0,5)$	$[w_\alpha + w_\gamma P_\gamma(0,4)/P_\alpha(0,4)]P_\alpha(0,5) + w_\beta P_\beta(0,5)$
...	...	...

Suppose that there are different trends in the P_α, P_β and P_γ indexes. Then comparing Table 2 with Table 3, it appears that the short term cell mean method of imputation will generally lead to more accurate estimates of the true Laspeyres indexes $\overline{P}_L(0,t)$ than the long term cell mean method of imputation studied in the previous section. It also appears that the short term cell mean indexes will be less prone to the bouncing phenomenon. However, if either of the P_β or P_γ price indexes have a trend that is divergent from the α trend, then it can be seen that the $P^{**}(0,t)$ indexes defined by (32) and (33) will still have some unwanted fluctuations. The reason is simple: if the trends are different, then the short run trend in the prices that are always available cannot capture the short run movement of the prices that are only intermittently available.

To formalize this intuition that the index $P^{**}(0,t)$ is less prone to bouncing behavior, define the period-to-period change in the index $P^{**}(0,t)$, measured *relative to* the always available commodities $P_\alpha(0,t)$, as:

$$(34) \qquad \Delta^{**}(t-1,t) \equiv [P^{**}(0,t)/P_\alpha(0,t) - P^{**}(0,t-1)/P_\alpha(0,t-1)] .$$

Then the following result compares these differences from the *short term* imputation method with the *long term* imputation method, as discussed in the previous section:

Proposition 2

Assume that $w_\beta = w_\gamma > 0$. Then, $|\Delta^{**}(t-1,t)| < |\Delta^*(t-2,t)|$.

Thus, under the simplifying assumption that $w_\beta = w_\gamma > 0$, we see that *absolute value of the one period* change $|\Delta^{**}(t-1,t)|$, obtained with the short term imputation method, is *strictly less than* the *absolute value of the two period* change $|\Delta^*(t-2,t)|$, obtained using the long term imputation. From Proposition 1, we know that the absolute value of the two period change is itself less than the highest of the absolute one period changes, when condition (25) holds. That is, the bouncing behavior using our long term imputation method is smoothed out when we compare across two periods, and we now see that using the short term imputation method the bouncing behavior is reduced even further!

Up to now, we have not used future information on price movements to help predict movements in current period prices. In the following section, we relax this restriction and use information on price quotes that are available in period t+1 to help us estimate the missing prices in period t. Obviously, this change in the admissible information set means that final estimates of price change for the current period cannot be made until the data from the following period has been collected. This limitation of the methods that will be proposed in the next section should be kept in mind.

5.   Interpolation Methods for Imputing Missing Prices

The methods of imputation that we propose in the present section estimate the missing price quotes for the current period using the movements in the same prices between the previous period and the succeeding period. Thus the methods that we discuss in this period are basically based on interpolating the missing prices and so we term these methods *interpolation methods* for imputing missing prices.

Our first interpolation method works as follows.   In period 1, we are missing the price information that would enable us to construct the Laspeyres index $P_\gamma(0,1)$ defined above by (10). The simplest hypothesis that we could make about the missing period 1 prices v_k^1 that are used to construct the missing index is that these prices have been growing at a *constant linear rate* going from period 0 to period 2. This simple hypothesis leads to the following imputed prices for the missing v_k^t for all odd periods t:[7]

$$(35) \quad v_k^{t***} \equiv [v_k^{t-1} + v_k^{t+1}]/2 ; \qquad\qquad k = 1,2,...,K ; t = 1,3,....$$

Using these imputed prices, the missing fixed base Laspeyres index for period t is estimated by:

$$(36) \quad \begin{aligned} P_\gamma^{***}(0,t) &\equiv \Sigma_{k=1}^K w_k^0 [v_k^{t***} / v_k^0] &\qquad t = 1,3,... \\ &= \Sigma_{k=1}^K w_k^0 \{[v_k^{t-1} + v_k^{t+1}] / 2v_k^0\} &\qquad \text{using (37)} \\ &= [P_\gamma(0,t-1) + P_\gamma(0,t+1)]/2 &\qquad \text{from (10).} \end{aligned}$$

where $P_\gamma(0,0) \equiv 1$. Similarly, imputed prices for the missing even period prices are defined as:

$$(37) \quad u_j^{t***} \equiv [u_j^{t-1} + u_j^{t+1}]/2 ; \qquad\qquad j = 1,2,...,J, t=2,4,6,...$$

Using these imputed prices, the missing fixed base Laspeyres index for even periods is estimated by:

$$(38) \quad \begin{aligned} P_\beta^{***}(0,t) &\equiv \Sigma_{j=1}^J w_j^0 [u_j^{t***} / u_j^0] \\ &= \Sigma_{j=1}^J w_j^0 \{[u_j^{t-1} + u_j^{t+1}] / 2u_j^0\} &\qquad \text{using (38)} \\ &= [P_\beta(0,t-1) + P_\beta(0,t+1)]/2 &\qquad \text{from (8).} \end{aligned}$$

Collecting the above estimators for the missing indexes, we see that if t is odd, we estimate the true long term Laspeyres index by the following index, which replaces the true $P_\gamma(0,t)$ by $P_\gamma^{***}(0,t)$:

$$(39) \quad P^{***}(0,t) \equiv w_\alpha P_\alpha(0,t) + w_\beta P_\beta(0,t) + w_\gamma[P_\gamma^{***}(0,t)] \qquad t = 1,3,5,...$$

$$= w_\alpha P_\alpha(0,t) + w_\beta P_\beta(0,t) + w_\gamma[P_\gamma(0,t-1) + P_\gamma(0,t+1)]/2$$

using (36) above. If t is even, we estimate the true long term Laspeyres index by the following index, which replaces the true $P_\beta(0,t)$ by $P_\beta^{***}(0,t)$:

$$(40) \quad P^{***}(0,t) \equiv w_\alpha P_\alpha(0,t) + w_\beta [P_\beta^{***}(0,t)] + w_\gamma P_\gamma(0,t) ; \qquad t = 2,4,6,...$$

$$= w_\alpha P_\alpha(0,t) + w_\beta[P_\beta(0,t-1) + P_\beta(0,t+1)]/2 + w_\gamma P_\gamma(0,t)$$

using (38) above.

---

[7] When t-1 equals 0, define v_k^0 by 1 for each index k.

The imputed indexes P***(0,t) can be compared to the true (but unobservable) sequence of Laspeyres indexes $\overline{P}_L(0,t)$ defined by (12) as follows:

Table 4: Linear Interpolated Laspeyres Indexes

Period	True index $\overline{P}_L(0,t)$	Imputed Index P*(0,t)
1	$w_\alpha P_\alpha(0,1) + w_\beta P_\beta(0,1) + w_\gamma P_\gamma(0,1)$	$w_\alpha P_\alpha(0,1) + w_\beta P_\beta(0,1) + w_\gamma[1+P_\gamma(0,2)]/2$
2	$w_\alpha P_\alpha(0,2) + w_\beta P_\beta(0,2) + w_\gamma P_\gamma(0,2)$	$w_\alpha P_\alpha(0,2) + w_\beta[P_\beta(0,1) + P_\beta(0,3)]/2 + w_\gamma P_\gamma(0,2)$
3	$w_\alpha P_\alpha(0,3) + w_\beta P_\beta(0,3) + w_\gamma P_\gamma(0,3)$	$w_\alpha P_\alpha(0,3) + w_\beta P_\beta(0,3) + w_\gamma[P_\gamma(0,2) + P_\gamma(0,4)]/2$
4	$w_\alpha P_\alpha(0,4) + w_\beta P_\beta(0,4) + w_\gamma P_\gamma(0,4)$	$w_\alpha P_\alpha(0,4) + w_\beta[P_\beta(0,3) + P_\beta(0,5)]/2 + w_\gamma P_\gamma(0,4)$
5	$w_\alpha P_\alpha(0,5) + w_\beta P_\beta(0,5) + w_\gamma P_\gamma(0,5)$	$w_\alpha P_\alpha(0,5) + w_\beta P_\beta(0,5) + w_\gamma[P_\gamma(0,4) + P_\gamma(0,4)]/2$
...	...	...

If the true P_β and P_γ indexes trend smoothly, it can be seen that the imputed indexes P***(0,t) will track the true Laspeyres indexes very closely, and the bouncing phenomenon will be eliminated entirely. Thus of the four methods of imputation that we have considered thus far, the present method based on simple linear interpolation seems best.

Obviously, there are additional variants of the methods we proposed in this section that could be studied. For example, instead of estimating the missing prices by taking arithmetic means of neighboring prices as in (35) and (37), we could use *geometric* means. In that case, the imputed prices in (35) and (37) would necessarily be lower, and so would the imputed price indexes in (39) and (40). We have used the arithmetic means here because it accords nicely with the Laspeyres formula for the long term indexes in (39) and (40): using the arithmetic mean of the *individual* prices for imputation is the same as using the arithmetic mean of the *missing indexes*. If instead the geometric formula was used for the price index, then we would strongly recommend using the geometric mean for the imputation of *individual* prices, as well. In that case, results analogous to (35)-(40) would hold, but with the prices replaced everywhere with the logarithm of prices.[8]

There is one situation (at least) where the simple interpolation methods proposed in this section will not give a satisfactory solution to the problem of missing price quotes. This is a situation where there is a great deal of variation in the general inflation rate going from period to period. For example, if the general inflation rate is accelerating rapidly (as in a hyperinflation), then the linear averaging that we have been advocating in this section will have the effect of *artificially raising* the previous period's overall index. Under these circumstances, the method suggested in

---

[8] Another possibility would be to use geometric averaging to define the imputed "micro" individual prices in (35) and (37), even though the Laspeyres indexes are used. We could contrast this with using geometric averaging to define the "macro" indexes in Laspeyres indexes in (38) and (40). Then it can be shown that using geometric averaging for the "micro" prices, followed by the existing definition in the first line of (38) or (40), will result in a *lower* overall index than instead using geometric averaging of the "macro" indexes in the second line of (38) or (40). This result is available in an earlier draft of the theoretical portion of this paper, entitled "Imputation using the Stochastic Approach to Index Numbers," Erwin Diewert and Robert Feenstra, March 2000.

15

the previous section may be more accurate. However, it is possible to design somewhat more complex interpolation schemes that will deal adequately with this situation of rapidly changing general inflation rates and we will now present such a design.

We will suppose that the general rate of inflation is captured by the price index $P_\alpha(0,t)$ constructed over the always available commodities. Then in order to impute any missing prices, we first divide the available prices in each period by $P_\alpha(0,t)$, so as to construct "real" prices. We then apply our methods in (35)-(40) above to these "real" prices.

Specially, this approach leads to the following imputed prices for the missing v_k^t for all odd periods t:[9]

$$(41) \quad v_k^{t****}/ P_\alpha(0,t) \equiv [v_k^{t-1}/ P_\alpha(0,t-1) + v_k^{t+1}/ P_\alpha(0,t+1)]/2 ; \qquad k = 1,2,...,K ; t =1,3,....$$

Using these imputed prices, the missing fixed base Laspeyres index for period t is estimated by:

$$(42) \quad P_\gamma****(0,t) \equiv \Sigma_{k=1}^K w_k^0 [v_k^{t****} / v_k^0] \qquad\qquad t = 1,3,...$$

$$= \Sigma_{k=1}^K w_k^0 \{[v_k^{t-1}/P_\alpha(0,t-1) + v_k^{t+1}/P_\alpha(0,t+1)] / 2v_k^0\}P_\alpha(0,t), \text{ using (41)}$$

$$= [P_\gamma(0,t-1) /P_\alpha(0,t-1) + P_\gamma(0,t+1) /P_\alpha(0,t+1)] P_\alpha(0,t)/2 , \qquad \text{from (10).}$$

where $P_\gamma(0,0) \equiv 1$. Similarly, imputed prices for the missing even period prices are defined as:

$$(43) \quad u_j^{t****}/P_\alpha(0,t) \equiv [u_j^{t-1}/P_\alpha(0,t-1) + u_j^{t+1}/P_\alpha(0,t+1)] /2 ; \qquad j = 1,2,...,J, t=2,4,6,...$$

Using these imputed prices, the missing fixed base Laspeyres index for even periods is estimated by:

$$(44) \quad P_\beta****(0,t) \equiv \Sigma_{j=1}^J w_j^0 [u_j^{t****} / u_j^0]$$

$$= \Sigma_{j=1}^J w_j^0 \{[u_j^{t-1}/P_\alpha(0,t-1) + u_j^{t+1}/P_\alpha(0,t+1)] / 2u_j^0\}P_\alpha(0,t) , \qquad \text{using (43)}$$

$$= [P_\beta(0,t-1) /P_\alpha(0,t-1) + P_\beta(0,t+1) /P_\alpha(0,t+1)] P_\alpha(0,t)/2 , \qquad \text{from (8).}$$

Thus, if t is odd, we estimate the true long term Laspeyres index by the following index, which replaces the true $P_\gamma(0,t)$ by $P_\gamma****(0,t)$:

$$(45) \quad P****(0,t) \equiv w_\alpha P_\alpha(0,t) + w_\beta P_\beta(0,t) + w_\gamma[P_\gamma****(0,t)], \qquad t = 1,3,5,...$$

---

[9] When t-1 equals 0, define v_k^0 by 1 for each index k.

If t is even, we estimate the true long term Laspeyres index by the following index, which replaces the true $P_\beta(0,t)$ by $P_\beta{****}(0,t)$:

$$(46) \quad P****(0,t) \equiv w_\alpha P_\alpha(0,t) + w_\beta [P_\beta****(0,t)] + w_\gamma P_\gamma(0,t) , \qquad t = 2,4,6,\ldots$$

So far, these formulas are all similar to what was obtained with the simple linear interpolation, except that all prices (or prices indexes) are first expressed in "real" terms by dividing by $P_\alpha(0,t)$.

To determine the properties of this more complex interpolation method, it is useful to express the index (46) in first differences *relative to* the always available commodities $P_\alpha(0,t)$, as:

$$(47) \quad \Delta****(t-1,t) \equiv [P****(0,t)/ P_\alpha(0,t) - P****(0,t-1)/ P_\alpha(0,t-1)] .$$

Then comparing this forward-looking imputation method with the short term cell mean method denoted by $\Delta**(t-1,t)$ defined in (34), we obtain:

Proposition 3

The linear interpolation of "real" prices results in an index that is a moving average of that obtained from the short term cell mean approach:

$$\Delta****(t-1,t) = [\Delta**(t-1,t) + \Delta**(t,t+1)]/2 .$$

Thus, the linear interpolation of "real" prices results in an index that will smooth out fluctuations obtained from the short term cell mean method. We already know that this latter method results in an index that is less erratic than either the long term cell mean imputation or not imputing at all, and now we see that using the linear interpolation of "real" prices will smooth the price index even more.

6. Dataset of International Prices

To investigate the various imputation techniques discussed above, we make use of a dataset from the International Price program (IPP) of BLS, which consists of all price quotes received during January 1997 to December 1999 at the most elementary "item" level. Included in this dataset was an indicator variable for whether each price quote is imputed or not. In the following sections, we will demonstrate the effects of alternative imputation procedures, including: simple carry-forward of previous prices; linear interpolation of missing prices; the short term cell mean approach, as currently done at IPP; and alternative cell mean approaches.[10] The criterion used to evaluate the imputation methods is to apply them to an *artificial* dataset in which some prices

---

[10] We will no longer consider the long term cell mean approach, since it was shown in section 3 that it is equivalent to not imputing at all. Thus, term "cell mean" will always refer to imputation of the short term price movement using the previous month's information, as in (28) and (30).

have been imputed, but the actual prices for these observations are known. Then the goal of the various methods will be to minimize the difference between the *actual* and *imputed* prices.

In Table 5, we show the fraction of observations in the original dataset that are imputed. There are 893,935 monthly observations at the elementary "item" level, over the three years of data. Of these, fully 34.4% are imputed, as shown in the first row. This fraction is higher than the *non-response rate* cited in the introduction, whereby 25.6% of the individual items tracked by the IPP do not report a price in any given month (though of these, about 60% eventually supply a price quote for that month or a later month). The reason for this discrepancy is that when an new item is added into the IPP survey (as occurs due to sample rotation or a genuinely new product), it will take several months before a questionnaire is sent to a company for that product. In the meantime, the price for the item is imputed, but it would *not be* considered a "non-response" to the questionnaire. In the dataset, there are 24,089 instances of new items being added, or 2.7% of the total number of observations. If it takes about three months to send out a questionnaire for a new product, then this would explain the difference between the imputation rate and the non-response rate.

Moving up, the first level of aggregation used by the is the "company-classification group." A "classification group" is similar to the Harmonized System, used to describe commodities in international trade, and consists of over 10,000 individual merchandise items. For some of these (such as automobiles), the IPP keeps track of the prices of multiple items from each of multiple companies. Thus, the price at the "company-classification group" level (e.g. a Ford car) is itself an Laspeyres index of the underlying item-level prices within this company (Ford) and classification group (cars of a certain size).[11]

At the "company-classification group" level, which has roughly one-half as many price observations. At this level, there are still 32.5% of the observations that are *comprised fully* of imputed item prices, as shown in the second row of Table 5. Next, we can go to the "classification group" level, which number 13,554 over both exports and imports. Counting these over the three years of data (which are not available for all classification groups), there are 147,082 observations in total. Of these, 18.9% are *fully comprised* of imputed item prices. Moving up from there, the next higher level of aggregation is the "lowest-level Enduse." The Enduse categories are a 5-digit classification used for the construction of GNP accounts by the Bureau of Economic Analysis. To these five digits, the IPP adds an additional classification "J" (judgmental) or "P" (probability).[12] At the level, the fraction of fully imputed observations now falls dramatically to 1.3%. These amount to 141 observations at various dates. Moving up to the 5-digit and 3-digit level (there is no separate 4-digit classification), the number of fully imputed observations drops to 114 and 15, respectively, and then is zero at even higher levels.

---

[11] The construction of the Laspeyres index at each level of aggregation is described fully in Alterman, Diewert and Feenstra (1999, chapter 6).

[12] The classification of "J" (judgmental) or "P" (probability) refers to how the sampling weights are derived; these weights are in turn used in the construction of the Laspeyres indexes.

Table 5: Imputed Observations in Original Dataset

	N	Fraction Imputed	Number Imputed
Item level	893,935	0.344	307,151
Company-classif. group	407,613	0.325	132,405
Classification group	147,082	0.189	27,835
Lower Enduse level (5-digit with J,P)	9,884	0.014	141
5-digit Enduse level	9,047	0.013	114
3-digit Enduse level	3,178	0.005	15

Table 6: Summary of Short-term Price Relatives, Original Dataset

N	Mean	Std Dev	Minimum	Maximum
Observation is not imputed, and lagged value is not imputed:				
513,654	0.9995361	0.0488687	0.0011622	6.0085437
Observation is imputed:				
283,062	0.9994038	0.0438278	0.2397446	4.3729739
Observation is not imputed, but the lagged value is imputed:				
73,130	1.0003046	0.0913728	0.0875208	4.3729739

Note: The observations above exclude those whose series is just beginning, in which case the corresponding STR is zero.

Of principle interest in the imputation is the behavior of the imputed prices, or what we define as the *short-term price relatives (STR):*

$$\text{(48)} \qquad\qquad STR_n^t = p_n^t/p_n^{t-1} , \qquad n=1,\dots,N.$$

Thus, the STR is simply the ratio of prices in two consecutive months.[13] In Table 6, we report the summary statistics for the *short-term price relatives (STRs)* at the elementary "item" level, for three groups of observations: (i) observations that are not imputed, and where the lagged value is also not imputed; (ii) observations that are imputed; (iii) observations that are not imputed, but which have the lagged value imputed. The third group is especially important, since these are the STR that are computed by making use of the lagged, imputed values. From Table 6, we see that the standard deviation of the STR for the first two groups are quite close, at 0.049 and 0.044, respectively. But the standard deviation for the third group is nearly twice as large, at 0.091. *This strongly suggests that computing the STR by using a lagged, imputed value introduces a significant amount of "noise" into the price movements.* Furthermore, notice that the mean values of the third group differs from the first two groups differ by at least 0.0008, which is 0.08% per month or 1% annually. In the theory we found that having different mean values for prices that imputed or not means that the imputation method may lead to erratic results.

7. Artificial Dataset

To investigate the effects of different imputation methods, an artificial dataset was created from the original set in the following steps:

(a) The original dataset was sorted by classification code, company code, item and date. Then all imputed observations were *deleted* (along with some observations with missing STR), which reduced the number of observations from 893,935 to 586,528;

(b) In this reduced set, successive observations were labeled "imputed" *in the same order* as in the original (sorted) dataset. For example, if the 10th-12th observations were imputed in the original set, then the 10th-12th were so labeled in the reduced set, etc.;

(c) The calendar dates in the original and artificial dataset are the same, i.e. the observation originally dated January 1998 will still be so dated in the artificial dataset, though this observation will be *missing* in the artificial set if it was *imputed* in the original.

To provide a simple example of an artificial dataset, suppose that there is just one item, available for one year. The data is sorted by months, and the original dataset contains imputed items in March-April, and August-September, as shown in Table 7.

---

[13] Actually, the item level prices p_{it} are first divided by some *base period* price p_n^0, obtaining a *long term relative* $LTR_n^t = p_n^t/p_n^0$, which is unit-free. Then the short term relative is obtained as $STR_n^t = LTR_n^t/LTR_n^{t-1}$.

Table 7: Example of Original and Artificial Datasets

Date	Original Prices	Imputed?	Artificial Prices	Imputed?
January	101		101	
February	103		103	
March	102	Yes	.	
April	106	Yes	.	
May	105		105	Yes
June	106		106	Yes
July	108		108	
August	110	Yes	.	
September	112	Yes	.	
October	115		115	
November	111		111	
December	109		109	Yes

Note:
The artificial dataset is created by omitting those observation that were imputed in the original dataset, and then labeling the remaining observation as "imputed" in the same order that these appeared in the original dataset.

To construct the artificial dataset, the first step is to delete the imputed observations for these fours months, as are shown in Table 7 with a period. Second, we label some observations as imputed. Since the 3rd-4th months, and 8th-9th months were imputed originally, we use this same ordering in the artificial dataset (while ignoring the deleted observations). This means that May-June are labeled as imputed, since these are the 3rd and 4th (non-missing) months, as well as December, which is the 8th (non-missing) month. If there was another item available, then the fact that September was imputed originally would mean that January, the first observation for the next item, would also be labeled as imputed.

The purpose of creating this artificial dataset will be to *temporarily omit* the price data for the observations that are labeled as "imputed," and then experiment with different procedures for imputing these values. In that way, the imputed values can be compared with the *actual* price values for these observations, to determine the accuracy of the imputation methods.

Before experimenting with any imputation procedures, we summarize properties of the artificial dataset in Tables 8 and 9, which are computed in the same manner as Tables 5 and 6. From Table 8, the number of imputed observations at the elementary "item" level is 34.5% in the artificial dataset, which is nearly identical to that in the original dataset. This is to be expected from the construction of the artificial dataset. At higher levels of aggregation, the fraction of imputed observations are also similar between Tables 5 and 8, except for some difference as the "company-classification group" level.

In Table 9, we report the summary statistics for the *short-term price relatives (STR)* of the artificial dataset at the elementary "item" level, again for three groups of observations: (i) observations that are not labeled as imputed, and where the lagged value is also not imputed; (ii) observations that are labeled as imputed; (iii) observations that are not imputed, but which have the lagged value labeled as imputed. The third group will have their item-level STR *recomputed* when we experiment with various imputation techniques. Before these calculations are done, however, it is of interest to see how the *true* STR in this third group compare with the first two groups. From Table 9, we see that the standard deviation of the STR in all three groups are quite similar, ranging between 0.047 and 0.51, and that the mean values are also very close. This contrasts sharply with Table 6, where the variance of the third group (with lagged imputed values) was *nearly twice as large* as the rest of the sample. Thus, in the artificial dataset, the *true* STR for observations that are label "imputed" are representative of the entire dataset, as we would expect by construction.

At the same time, there are some differences between the original and artificial datasets that we should highlight. Because the artificial set *omits* all the imputed observations and also labels other observations as "imputed", it will tend to have *more months between non-missing, non-imputed observations* than the original dataset. This can be seen from the example shown in Table 7, where the original dataset has imputed prices in March-April, and August-September. Then the artificial dataset has missing prices for March and April, and the prices in May and June are labeled as imputed, so there are *five* months from the prices in February to those in July, whereas in the original dataset there are just *three* months from prices in February those in May.

Table 8: Imputed Observations in Artificial Dataset

	N	Fraction Imputed	Number Imputed
Item level	586,528	0.345	202,622
Company-classif. group	275,208	0.233	64,216
Classification group	119,247	0.169	20,127
Lower Enduse level (5-digit with J,P)	9,743	0.017	162
5-digit Enduse level	8,933	0.014	128
3-digit Enduse level	3,163	0.008	26

Table 9: Summary of *True* Short-term Price Relatives, Artificial Dataset

N	Mean	Std Dev	Minimum	Maximum
Observation is not imputed, and lagged value is not imputed:				
292,236	0.9995505	0.0498350	0.0094737	5.8791209
Observation is labeled imputed:				
177,781	0.9994585	0.0466720	0.0011622	3.7586207
Observation is not imputed, but the lagged value is labeled imputed:				
43,637	0.9997559	0.0510347	0.2290744	6.0085437

This aspect of the original and artificial datasets is described in Table 10, where we show the frequency distribution of the number of months T between *non-missing, non-imputed observations* (ignoring cases where T=1, meaning that there are no imputed observations between two successive months). The average value of T is 3.25 for the original dataset, and 4.21 for the artificial dataset. More generally, the values of the cumulative frequency distribution for T in the original dataset is everywhere above that for the artificial dataset, i.e. for each value of T, there are more observations in the original set have that many months or fewer lying between non-imputed observations.

Aside from this feature, there may well be other differences between the two datasets that we are not able to measure. Suppose, for instance, that the imputed observations in the original dataset occur for some economic reasons, e.g. prices have not changed, so the companies do not send in the reporting forms. Then the true (but unobserved) behavior of these prices would be quite different from those in the artificial dataset that we have labeled "imputed." We have no way to assess or control for these differences between the datasets, and this can be viewed as a limitation of our analysis.[14]

We now investigate whether imputation methods applied to the artificial dataset lead to "nosier" STR in this third group of observations, where the lagged values are imputed.

8. Carry-forward and Linear Interpolation of Price Observations

The first, and simplest, imputation method is to carry forward the previous values of the price until a new value is collected. Suppose that this new value is available in month t, and that the previous value was available in month t-T, with $T \geq 2$. Using this method, we can construct two different measures of the accuracy of this "carry forward" technique:

$$(49) \qquad STRCARRY_n^t = p_n^t / p_n^{t-T}$$

$$(50) \qquad DIFCARRY_n^t = | p_n^{t-1} - p_n^{t-T}|/ p_n^{t-1}, \quad T \geq 2.$$

The first of these measures, STRCARRY, gives the short term relative that would result by carrying forward the value p_n^{t-T} to period t-1, and then comparing this price to p_n^t. This short term relative can be compared to those reported in Table 6 when the observation is not imputed, but the lagged value is labeled "imputed". Specifically, we found in Table 6 that the STR when the lagged values where imputed were *twice as variable* as the STR in the rest of the dataset. We will be interested in seeing whether this is also true for STRCARRY.

---

[14] We are indebted to Katharine Abraham for pointing out this limitation.

Table 10: Time between Non-imputed Observations, Original and Artificial Datasets

	Original Data		Artificial Data	
Months	Frequency	Cumulative Percent	Frequency	Cumulative Percent
2	19587	42.33	11105	29.68
3	16806	78.66	11414	60.19
4	3593	86.42	4387	71.91
5	1538	89.75	2702	79.13
6	1915	93.89	2509	85.84
7	803	95.62	1325	89.38
8	471	96.64	866	91.69
9	540	97.81	812	93.86
10	252	98.35	470	95.12
11	170	98.72	365	96.10
12	249	99.26	363	97.07
13	89	99.45	211	97.63
14	60	99.58	163	98.06
15	49	99.68	172	98.52
16	30	99.75	121	98.85
17	20	99.79	84	99.07
18	42	99.88	89	99.31
19	22	99.93	61	99.47
20	9	99.95	43	99.59
21	3	99.96	45	99.71
22	3	99.96	22	99.77
23	6	99.98	22	99.83
24	0	99.98	17	99.87
25	1	99.98	9	99.90
26	1	99.98	15	99.94
27	8	100.00	8	99.96
28	0	100.00	8	99.98
29	0	100.00	4	99.99
31	1	100.00	2	99.99
32			1	100.00
33			1	100.00

Mean: Original data = 3.25 months, Artificial data = 4.21 months

The other measure, DIFCARRY, takes the absolute value of the difference between the *actual and imputed price* in the last month of the imputation, expressed relative to the actual price. Like STRCARRY, we construct this criterion in months when the observation is not imputed, but the lagged value is labeled "imputed". In addition, we shall consider the values of DIFCARRY for up to *three months* before the last non-imputed price, as follows:

$$(51) \qquad DIF2CARRY_n^t = |\, p_n^{t-2} - p_n^{t-T}|/\, p_n^{t-2}, \qquad T \geq 3,$$

$$(52) \qquad DIF3CARRY_n^t = |\, p_n^{t-3} - p_n^{t-T}|/\, p_n^{t-3}, \qquad T \geq 4.$$

The second imputation method is to linearly interpolate the item-level prices between the previous value of the price, and the new value that is collected. Suppose that the last available data was $T \geq 2$ months ago. Then the prices are linearly interpolated according to the formula:

$$(53) \qquad LINEAR_n^{t-i} = p_n^{t-T} + (T-i)(p_n^t - p_n^{t-T})/T, \quad i=1,2,\ldots,T.$$

where: $LINEAR_n^{t-i}$ = the interpolated price for the ith month *before* the current month; p_n^{t-T} = the price for the last month (t-T) with price data that is not labeled "imputed"; p_n^t = the current price. Again, we can construct two different measures of the accuracy of the interpolation technique:

$$(54) \qquad STRLIN_n^t = p_n^t / LINEAR_n^{t-1}$$

$$(55) \qquad DIFLIN_n^t = |\, p_n^{t-1} - LINEAR_n^{t-1}| /p_n^{t-1}, \qquad T \geq 2.$$

The interpretations of these two criterion for linear interpolation is similar to their interpretation for the carry-forward technique. STRLIN in (54) gives the short-term relative computed between the last month of linear interpolation, and the next month of actual price data. We are interested in seeing whether the standard deviation of this criterion is exceptionally large. DIFLIN in (55) gives the absolute value of the difference between the *actual and imputed price* in the last month of the imputation, expressed relative to the actual price. Like STRLIN, we construct this criterion in months when the observation is not imputed, but the lagged value is labeled "imputed". In addition, we shall consider the values of DIFLIN for up to *three months* before the last non-imputed price, as follows:

$$(56) \qquad DIF2LIN_n^t = |\, p_n^{t-2} - LINEAR_n^{t-2}| /p_n^{t-2}, \qquad T \geq 3,$$

$$(57) \qquad DIF3LIN_n^t = |\, p_n^{t-3} - LINEAR_n^{t-3}| /p_n^{t-3}, \qquad T \geq 4.$$

The results of the first two imputation techniques, computed over all observations in the artificial dataset, are reported in Table 11.

Table 11: Summary of Carry-forward and Linear Interpolation

Variable	N	Mean	Std Dev	Minimum	Maximum

(A) Exports

Short-term relative between imputed and non-imputed price:

Variable	N	Mean	Std Dev	Minimum	Maximum
STRTRUE	21864	0.9996778	0.0440504	0.3272171	3.0000000
STRCARRY	18878	0.9983707	0.0959513	0.2280000	6.0000000
STRLIN	18878	0.9982478	0.0243143	0.5034965	1.4835681

Differences between actual and imputed prices (in percent):

Variable	N	Mean	Std Dev	Minimum	Maximum
DIFCARRY	17636	0.0232519	0.0844687	0	3.2967914
DIFLIN	17636	0.0103225	0.0363065	0	0.9861111
DIF2CARRY	11104	0.0219724	0.0808387	0	3.2967914
DIF2LIN	11104	0.0133111	0.0419300	0	1.0989305
DIF3CARRY	5523	0.0282794	0.0985733	0	3.2967914
DIF3LIN	5523	0.0190500	0.0618059	0	1.6483957

(B) Imports

Short-term relative between imputed and non-imputed price:

Variable	N	Mean	Std Dev	Minimum	Maximum
STRTRUE	21709	0.9997205	0.0558301	0.2290744	6.0085437
STRCARRY	18428	0.9964100	0.0927185	0.2219646	4.1176484
STRLIN	18428	0.9980984	0.0244097	0.5094340	1.5384615

Differences between actual and imputed prices (in percent):

Variable	N	Mean	Std Dev	Minimum	Maximum
DIFCARRY	17190	0.0255967	0.0919111	0	5.0085687
DIFLIN	17190	0.0117618	0.0541308	0	5.0085499
DIF2CARRY	11245	0.0236498	0.0839319	0	3.5052224
DIF2LIN	11245	0.0152113	0.0483392	0	2.0000001
DIF3CARRY	5307	0.0272394	0.0901576	0	3.5052224
DIF3LIN	5307	0.0185398	0.0455863	0	0.7908163

Note: These calculations are done over observations in the artificial dataset that are not imputed, but have their lagged value imputed.

Part (A) of Table 11 deals with exports, and part (B) deals with imports. We report first the mean values of the STR, computed for those observations that are not imputed, but whose lagged value is labeled as "imputed". The *true* value of the STR, indicated by STRTRUE, has a standard deviation of 0.044 for exports and 0.056 for imports. In contrast, the STR using the carry-forward technique, indicated by STRCARRY, has a standard deviation which is nearly twice as large, at 0.096 for exports and 0.093 for imports. Recall that when considering the observations in the *original* dataset that are not imputed, but have their lagged value imputed, we also obtained an STR with standard deviation that was twice as large as the rest of the sample (see the last row of Table 6). The original dataset used a short term cell mean method of imputation, so in this respect the carry-forward technique performs quite similarly. In contrast, the linear interpolation results in a standard deviation for the STR, indicated by STRLIN, that is about *one-half* of its true value, for either exports or imports. In this sense, the linear interpolation leads to *even less* month-to-month volatility in prices than the true data.

The remaining rows of Table 11, parts (A) and (B), report the absolute value of the percentage difference between the *imputed* and *actual* prices, during the last three months of imputation. In the first month before the non-imputed price, the carry-forward technique has a value of DIFCARRY=0.023 or 2.3% for exports, while for the linear interpolation we obtain DIFLIN=0.010 or 1.0%. Similar magnitudes are obtained for imports, where the carry-forward technique differs from the true prices by more than twice as much as with linear interpolation. However, as we work backwards in the months, the relative difference between these two imputation techniques is reduced. In the second and third lagged month of imputation, for either exports or imports, the carry-forward technique differs from the true prices by about 50% more than the linear interpolation.

In a separate Appendix, we report the results from these two techniques, summarizing the means and standard deviations at the one-digit Enduse level. The results are similar to what we have found for total exports and imports.

One problem with the linear interpolation technique is that it would be difficult to implement in practice when $T > 3$, that is, when there is more than three months between actual price observations. The reason for this is that the IPP keeps price data up and running for only the current and three lagged months, so that computing (57) when $T > 3$ would not be feasible. A solution to this problem is to use the carry-forward technique *initially*, but then revert to the linear interpolation with (at most) a three month lag when an actual price quote is obtained for any item. That is, we define a *hybrid* measure of the imputed price as:

$$= \text{LINEAR}_n^{t-i} \text{ if } i \leq T \leq 3,$$

$$(58) \qquad \text{LINCARRY}_n^{t-i} = p_n^{t-T} \text{ if } 3 < i \leq T,$$

$$= p_n^{t-T} + (3-i)(p_n^t - p_n^{t-3})/3, \text{ if } i \leq 3 < T.$$

Operationally, this would mean that the IPP staff carries forward the last value of a price until a new quote is collected. If there is *three or less* months between quotes, then the linear interpolation technique is used to "fill in" the missing prices – as in the first line of (58). If there is *more than three* months between quotes, then the previous value of the price is used for all months before the (current and) last three – as in the second line of (58). For the last three months, the IPP staff revise the published indexes by interpolating this item in a linear fashion between its lagged value p_n^{t-T} and its current value p_n^t – as expressed in the last line of (58). Thus, only the indexes published during the *past quarter* would be subject to revision. Given this third technique, we assess it validity in the same way as the other two methods:

$$(59) \qquad STRLINC_t = p_n^t \, / \, LINCARRY_n^{t-1} ,$$

$$(60) \qquad DLINCAR_n^{t-1} = | \, p_n^{t-1} - LINCARRY_n^{t-1} | / \, p_n^{t-1}, \qquad T \geq 2,$$

$$(61) \qquad D2LINCAR_n^{t-1} = | \, p_n^{t-2} - LINCARRY_n^{t-2} | / \, p_n^{t-2}, \qquad T \geq 3,$$

$$(62) \qquad D3LINCAR_n^{t-1} = | \, p_n^{t-3} - LINCARRY_n^{t-3} | / \, p_n^{t-3}, \qquad T \geq 4.$$

In Table 12, we report the absolute value of the percentage difference between the imputed and actual prices, for the *hybrid* technique and the previous linear interpolation technique. Again, part (A) deals with exports and part (B) deals with imports. In the first month before the non-imputed price, the linear interpolation gives DIFLIN=0.010 or 1.0% for exports, while for the *hybrid* technique we obtain a value of DLINCAR=0.012 or 1.2%. Similar values are obtained for imports. Thus, the linear interpolation results in imputed prices that are slightly closer to their true values, but not by much as compared to the hybrid technique. As we work backwards in the months, the difference between these two imputation methods increases somewhat. In the second lagged month before each non-imputed price, the linear interpolation gives DIF2LIN=0.013 or 1.3%, while the *hybrid* technique gives D2LINCAR=0.017 or 1.7%. In the third lagged month before each non-imputed price, we obtain DIF3LIN=0.019 or 1.9% from the linear interpolation, while for the *hybrid* technique we have D3LINCAR=0.028 or 2.8%, with similar values for imports. In this third lagged month, the hybrid technique is identical to carry-forward, and its deviation from the true prices is about 50% greater than that obtained with the linear interpolation.

In the Appendix, we report the results at the one-digit Enduse level, which generally show the same pattern as in Table 12. That is, the hybrid technique results in differences from the true prices that somewhat *exceed* that obtained from the linear interpolation, but the difference between these two imputation methods is not that great in the first lagged month. By the third lagged month, the hybrid technique is identical to carry-forward, and its deviation from the true prices is about 50% to 100% greater than that obtained with the linear interpolation.

Table 12: Summary of Hybrid Technique and Linear Interpolation

Variable	N	Mean	Std Dev	Minimum	Maximum

(A) Exports

Short-term relative between imputed and non-imputed price:

Variable	N	Mean	Std Dev	Minimum	Maximum
STRTRUE	21864	0.9996778	0.0440504	0.3272171	3.0000000
STRLIN	18878	0.9982478	0.0243143	0.5034965	1.4835681
STRLINCAR	18878	0.9975962	0.0322332	0.4697802	1.4835681

Differences between actual and imputed prices (in percent):

Variable	N	Mean	Std Dev	Minimum	Maximum
DIFLIN	17636	0.0103225	0.0363065	0	0.9861111
DLINCAR	17636	0.0120494	0.0393572	0	1.0989305
DIF2LIN	11104	0.0133111	0.0419300	0	1.0989305
D2LINCAR	11104	0.0173358	0.0564909	0	2.1978610
DIF3LIN	5523	0.0190500	0.0618059	0	1.6483957
D3LINCAR	5523	0.0282794	0.0985733	0	3.2967914

(B) Imports

Short-term relative between imputed and non-imputed price:

Variable	N	Mean	Std Dev	Minimum	Maximum
STRTRUE	21709	0.9997205	0.0558301	0.2290744	6.0085437
STRLIN	18428	0.9980984	0.0244097	0.5094340	1.5384615
STRLINCAR	18428	0.9970780	0.0318351	0.4611679	1.5384615

Differences between actual and imputed prices (in percent):

Variable	N	Mean	Std Dev	Minimum	Maximum
DIFLIN	17190	0.0117618	0.0541308	0	5.0085499
DLINCAR	17190	0.0134164	0.0555605	0	5.0085520
DIF2LIN	11245	0.0152113	0.0483392	0	2.0000001
D2LINCAR	11245	0.0189168	0.0593021	0	2.3368150
DIF3LIN	5307	0.0185398	0.0455863	0	0.7908163
D3LINCAR	5307	0.0272394	0.0901576	0	3.5052224

Note: These calculations are done over observations in the artificial dataset that are not imputed, but have their lagged value imputed.

9.   Short Term Cell Mean Imputation

The next method is to imputed values using the short term cell mean approach, as described in section 4, much as is currently done by the IPP.[15] In this technique, the Laspeyres-ratio index is computed from the artificial dataset, *without using any of the price data labeled as "imputed,"* at each of following levels of aggregation: (i) company-classification group; (ii) classification group; (iii) 5-digit Enduse (including J and P); (iv) 5-digit Enduse classification; (v) 3-digit Enduse classification; (vi) 2-digit Enduse classification.

Using these results, whenever a *short-term relative (STR)* is either labeled as imputed in the artificial dataset, or is missing, then it is *replaced* by the Laspeyres-ratio index computed at the lowest possible level of aggregation. For example, if the STR for some item is labeled as imputed, then we first check whether the same *company-classification group* has a Laspeyres-ratio computed. This Laspeyres-ratio will be available if the same company and classification group has some price data that is *not labeled as imputed* in the same month, and the preceding month. If so, then that STR is replaced with the Laspeyres-ratio. If not, then we check whether the same *classification group* has a Laspeyres-ratio computed; if so, then that STR is replaced with the Laspeyres-ratio. If not, then we check whether the same *5-digit Enduse group* has a Laspeyres-ratio computed; if so, then that STR is replaced with the Laspeyres-ratio. This procedure continues until we have worked up to the 2-digit Enduse level, at which time all observations labeled as imputed, or missing, will be "filled in" by the cell-mean method.

Following this, the price for the observations labeled as imputed is re-computed as:

(63) $PCELL_n^t = p_n^{t-1} * STR_n^t$, if observation t-1 is not imputed;

(64) $PCELL_n^t = PCELL_n^{t-1} * STR_n^t$,   if observation t-1 and t are both imputed

That is, we re-compute the prices by cumulating the imputed STR, in the same manner as is currently performed within the IPP.   The accuracy of this "cell mean" technique can be assessed using similar statistics to what we have already considered:

(65) $STRCELL_n^t = p_n^t / PCELL_n^{t-1}$

(66) $DIFCELL_n^t = | p_n^{t-1} - PCELL_n^{t-1}|/ p_n^{t-1}$, $T \geq 2$,

(67) $DIF2CELL_n^t = | p_n^{t-2} - PCELL_n^{t-2}|/ p_n^{t-2}$, $T \geq 3$,

(68) $DIF3CELL_n^t = | p_n^{t-3} - PCELL_n^{t-3}|/ p_n^{t-3}$, $T \geq 4$.

---

[15]   In note 6 we described several differences between the short term cell mean approach of section 4, and actual IPP procedures. The short term cell mean approach that we empirically implement in this section is identical to IPP procedures, so it differs in those respects from the theoretical description of section 4.

The results are shown in Table 13. The first measure reported, STRCELL, gives the short-term relative that would result by using the cell-mean technique. This criterion can be compared to those reported in Table 6 when the observation is not imputed, but the lagged value is labeled "imputed". Specifically, we found in Table 6 that the STR when the lagged values where imputed were *twice as variable* as the STR in the rest of the dataset. In Table 13, looking at exports in part (A), we find that the standard deviation of STRCELL=0.094 is more than *twice* the standard deviation of STRTRUE=0.044, which is the STR using actual prices. For imports in part (B), the standard deviation of STRCELL=0.086 is slightly less than twice the standard deviation using actual prices, STRTRUE=0.056. Thus, applying the cell-mean method to the artificial dataset results in short-term relatives that are "too noisy," when measured in the first month that a price not labeled as imputed becomes available.

Next, we can compare the difference between actual and imputed prices using the cell-mean and hybrid imputation techniques. DIFCELL=0.023 and DLINCAR=0.012 give these differences in the first lag before each non-imputed price, for exports, and we see that the cell-mean method gives an average difference which is about *twice as high* as for the hybrid technique. The same holds for imports. In the second lag, DIF2CELL is still slightly higher than D2LINCAR, but by the third lag this difference between the two techniques has reversed, for either exports or imports. In other words, the cell-mean is slightly closer to actual prices than is the hybrid technique in the third lag (the hybrid technique is equivalent to carry-forward in the third lag), but the cell-mean does worse than the hybrid technique in the second and first lags. In summary, the cell mean technique, as currently used by the IPP and other programs at BLS, dominates the hybrid technique only slightly in the third lag.

In the Appendix we report the results at the one-digit Enduse level, which generally show the same pattern as in Table 13. That is, the cell-mean technique results in differences from the true prices that somewhat *exceed* that obtained from the hybrid interpolation in the first and second lag, but the difference between these two imputation methods is small (and in either direction) in the third lag.

10.   Combining the Cell Mean and Linear Interpolation

In section 5, we suggested combining the cell mean and linear interpolations, whereby the "real" prices were interpolated. This would recommended during periods of rapidly changing, or highly erratic, prices. There is another more practical reason to combine these techniques. As we have already noted, the IPP program keeps data for only 3 months, so that doing a linear interpolation between the current and last price quote might not be feasible. One solution to this problem was the hybrid technique discussed in section 8, whereby the prices are simply carried forward, and then a linear interpolation over three months (or less) is performed when a new quote is available. An *alternative* hybrid technique would be to impute the prices using the short term cell mean method, and then apply a linear interpolation over three months (or less) when a new quote is available. These two hybrid techniques differ only in terms of the method to impute the prices *before* the linear interpolation is applied, and they are referred to as LINCAR for the first hybrid, combining the carry-forward with linear interpolation, and LINCELL for the second hybrid, combining the cell-mean with linear interpolation. Both these methods are practical alternatives to the imputation currently done by IPP.

Table 13: Summary of Cell Mean and Hybrid Imputations

Variable	N	Mean	Std Dev	Minimum	Maximum

(A) Exports

Short-term relative between imputed and non-imputed price:

Variable	N	Mean	Std Dev	Minimum	Maximum
STRTRUE	21864	0.9996778	0.0440504	0.3272171	3.0000000
STRCELL	17057	1.0013562	0.0936856	0.2926829	6.8796068
STRLINCAR	18878	0.9975962	0.0322332	0.4697802	1.4835681

Differences between actual and imputed prices (in percent):

Variable	N	Mean	Std Dev	Minimum	Maximum
DIFCELL	17057	0.0228482	0.0785664	0	2.4166667
DLINCAR	17636	0.0120494	0.0393572	0	1.0989305
DIF2CELL	10664	0.0202748	0.0701460	0	2.4166667
D2LINCAR	11104	0.0173358	0.0564909	0	2.1978610
DIF3CELL	5297	0.0254721	0.0829550	0	2.4166667
D3LINCAR	5523	0.0282794	0.0985733	0	3.2967914

(B) Imports

Short-term relative between imputed and non-imputed price:

Variable	N	Mean	Std Dev	Minimum	Maximum
STRTRUE	21709	0.9997205	0.0558301	0.2290744	6.0085437
STRCELL	16597	1.0022704	0.0857781	0.2302684	3.1609195
STRLINCAR	18428	0.9970780	0.0318351	0.4611679	1.5384615

Differences between actual and imputed prices (in percent):

Variable	N	Mean	Std Dev	Minimum	Maximum
DIFCELL	16597	0.0254358	0.0769573	0	2.9319156
DLINCAR	17190	0.0134164	0.0555605	0	5.0085520
DIF2CELL	10785	0.0233514	0.0771853	0	2.9319156
D2LINCAR	11245	0.0189168	0.0593021	0	2.3368150
DIF3CELL	5082	0.0270413	0.0810556	0	2.9319156
D3LINCAR	5307	0.0272394	0.0901576	0	3.5052224

Note: These calculations are done over observations in the artificial dataset that are not imputed, but have their lagged value imputed.

We have applied both hybrid techniques, with results shown in Table 14. Comparing the STR of the two hybrid techniques, or the differences with actual prices in the first, second or third lag, the two techniques give remarkably similar results! In the first lag, for example, we obtain DLINCELL = 0.0110 and DLINCAR = 0.0109 for exports, and DLINCELL = 0.0124 and DLINCAR = 0.0122 for exports. The differences with actual prices continue to be very similar across the two techniques in the second and third lags.[16] Thus, if linear interpolation is going to be performed over a three-month window, then it goes not make much difference whether the prices *before* this time simply have their former values carried forward, or are imputed using the cell mean technique. Either of these hybrid techniques are preferable to using carry-forward or cell-mean without any linear interpolation. These conclusion also holds at the one-digit Enduse level, as reported in the Appendix, where the difference between the two hybrid techniques is small and of either sign.

11.   Using Country of Origin/Destination

A final method we will investigate is to impute the missing prices using data from *the same country of origin or destination*, and within the closest product group. This approach might be most relevant for *imports*, where commodities from the same country of origin are faced with identical exchange rate movement, but we also apply the technique to U.S. *exports*, distinguishing their country of destination. Under this approach, the Laspeyres-ratio index is computed from the artificial dataset at each of following levels of aggregation: (i) same country of origin/destination and same classification group; (ii) same country of origin/ destination and same 5-digit Enduse (including J and P); (iii) same country of origin/destination and same 5-digit Enduse classification; (iv) same country of origin/destination and same 3-digit Enduse classification; (v) same country of origin/destination and same 2-digit Enduse classification; (vi) same country of origin/destination and same 1-digit Enduse classification. Whenever a price is missing, it is imputed using the calculated index at the lowest level of aggregation on this tree.

With this difference in the imputation method, all our other calculations are much the same as what we performed above. Thus, Table 15 compares the hybrid calculation – linear interpolation over three months with initial carry-forward – with the cell mean using the same country of origin or destination. These results can be contrasted with Table 13, where we showed the hybrid calculation and the cell mean imputation computed over the nearest product group (but not using country of origin or destination). By construction, the hybrid calculations in the two tables give identical results, while it is the cell-mean imputations that differ in principle. But surprisingly, the results for the cell-mean imputations of Table 13 and 15 are nearly the same! Noting that the number of observations used to compute the various statistics differ slightly (due to complexities of the calculations), there is hardly any observable difference between using country of origin/destination in imputing prices, and not using this information. Perhaps differences between these techniques would show up at a disaggregate level, but such differences are not pronounced enough to show up for total exports and imports.

---

[16] It should be noted that the number of observations in the dataset when the two hybrid methods are combined is slightly less than in previous tables, so the values change slightly.

Table 14: Summary of Two Hybrid Techniques

Variable	N	Mean	Std Dev	Minimum	Maximum
(A) Exports					
Short-term relative between imputed and non-imputed price:					
STRTRUE	21791	0.9997182	0.0440231	0.3272171	3.0000000
STRLINCELL	16046	0.9983748	0.0288780	0.5034965	1.4835681
STRLINCAR	16046	0.9981244	0.0293817	0.5034965	1.4835681
Differences between actual and imputed prices (in percent):					
DLINCELL	16046	0.0110036	0.0364708	0	0.9861111
DLINCAR	16046	0.0109011	0.0361675	0	0.9861111
D2LINCELL	10225	0.0155947	0.0499423	0	1.6111111
D2LINCAR	10225	0.0152773	0.0485795	0	1.2474527
D3LINCELL	5034	0.0251831	0.0842361	0	2.4166667
D3LINCAR	5034	0.0248022	0.0827719	0	1.6097272
(B) Imports					
Short-term relative between imputed and non-imputed price:					
STRTRUE	21624	0.9997204	0.0559372	0.2290744	6.0085437
STRLINCELL	15637	0.9983146	0.0289353	0.4729803	1.5384615
STRLINCAR	15637	0.9976540	0.0291785	0.4611679	1.5384615
Differences between actual and imputed prices (in percent):					
DLINCELL	15637	0.0123671	0.0363499	0	1.1564735
DLINCAR	15637	0.0121537	0.0371566	0	1.1684075
D2LINCELL	10410	0.0178335	0.0542632	0	1.9546104
D2LINCAR	10410	0.0171933	0.0557163	0	2.3368150
D3LINCELL	4871	0.0262851	0.0806930	0	2.9319156
D3LINCAR	4871	0.0244013	0.0857199	0	3.5052224

Note: These calculations are done over observations in the artificial dataset that are not imputed, but have their lagged value imputed.

Table 15: Summary of Cell Mean and Hybrid Imputations
-- Using Country of Origin/Destination

Variable	N	Mean	Std Dev	Minimum	Maximum

(A) Exports

Short-term relative between imputed and non-imputed price:

Variable	N	Mean	Std Dev	Minimum	Maximum
STRTRUE	21864	0.9996778	0.0440504	0.3272171	3.0000000
STRCELL	15746	1.0011048	0.0892516	0.2926829	6.8796068
STRLINCAR	18878	0.9975962	0.0322332	0.4697802	1.4835681

Differences between actual and imputed prices (in percent):

Variable	N	Mean	Std Dev	Minimum	Maximum
DIFCELL	15746	0.0239274	0.0738378	0	2.4166667
DLINCAR	17636	0.0120494	0.0393572	0	1.0989305
DIF2CELL	10037	0.0218265	0.0656893	0	1.6529557
D2LINCAR	11104	0.0173358	0.0564909	0	2.1978610
DIF3CELL	4939	0.0272895	0.0756754	0	1.3578140
D3LINCAR	5523	0.0282794	0.0985733	0	3.2967914

(B) Imports

Short-term relative between imputed and non-imputed price:

Variable	N	Mean	Std Dev	Minimum	Maximum
STRTRUE	21707	0.9997204	0.0558327	0.2290744	6.0085437
STRCELL	15416	1.0015277	0.0814531	0.2328672	3.8014859
STRLINCAR	18428	0.9970780	0.0318351	0.4611679	1.5384615

Differences between actual and imputed prices (in percent):

Variable	N	Mean	Std Dev	Minimum	Maximum
DIFCELL	15416	0.0252304	0.0769434	0	2.9847505
DLINCAR	17190	0.0134164	0.0555605	0	5.0085520
DIF2CELL	10267	0.0235915	0.0773548	0	2.9928985
D2LINCAR	11245	0.0189168	0.0593021	0	2.3368150
DIF3CELL	4793	0.0274864	0.0802594	0	2.9997446
D3LINCAR	5307	0.0272394	0.0901576	0	3.5052224

Note: These calculations are done over observations in the artificial dataset that are not imputed, but have their lagged value imputed.

In Table 16 we also report the results from comparing the two hybrid techniques: linear interpolation of three months with cell-mean before this, and linear interpolation of three months with initial carry-forward. These results can be contrasted with Table 14, where the cell-mean did not use any information on country of origin or destination. Except for some differences in the number of observations in Table 14, the results for linear interpolation with initial carry-forward are identical across Tables 13 – 16, by construction. But in addition, the results for the linear interpolation with initial cell-mean are nearly identical in Tables 14 and 16. In other words, we again find that using the information on country of origin or destination has hardly any impact on our results, at least not at the level of total exports and imports.

In the Appendix we report the results at the one-digit Enduse level, which generally show the same pattern as in Table 13 – 16. That is, the cell-mean technique gives results that are quite similar whether the country of origin/destination is used, or not. In one case (Enduse Q3), using the country of destination for the cell-mean resulted in an imputation that was noticeably *further* away from the true prices, and in no case did the use of this information appear to significantly improve the imputation.

12.   Conclusions

The issue of imputing prices used to construct official price indexes has been largely ignored in the literature, and together with Armknecht and Maitland-Smith (1999), this paper begins to fill that gap. Our theoretical exploration has led us through four imputation techniques: the long term cell mean method (which turned out to be equivalent to not imputing); the short term cell mean method (currently used by the IPP and other programs at BLS); linear interpolation; and linear interpolation using "real" prices (i.e. deflated by the cell mean of other available prices). In a somewhat different order, we have empirically examined five techniques: simple carry-forward of prices; linear interpolation; a hybrid technique that combines these two; short term cell mean imputation; and a hybrid technique that combines cell mean with linear interpolation. From the theory and empirical results, our conclusions can be summarized as follows:

1) *Some imputation is better than no imputation:*
    Without imputation, the price index is likely to be "noisy" due to changing commodity sets in each period, or will exclude a great deal of information if the set of commodities is restricted to be the same over time. Both of these alternatives is undesirable, making some form of imputation essential for statistical agencies.

2) *The short term cell mean introduces some "noise" into the price index:*
    While the short term cell mean method, as is currently practiced, is better than no imputation, there are strong theoretical reasons to expect this method to result in undue fluctuation in the price index. This was strongly confirmed in the empirical work, where the short term relative computed over observations that were not imputed, but had their lagged value imputed, was nearly *twice as variable* as the rest of the sample.

Table 16: Summary of Two Hybrid Techniques
-- Using Country of Origin/Destination

Variable	N	Mean	Std Dev	Minimum	Maximum

(A) Exports

Short-term relative between imputed and non-imputed price:

Variable	N	Mean	Std Dev	Minimum	Maximum
STRTRUE	21864	0.9996778	0.0440504	0.3272171	3.0000000
STRLINCELL	16290	0.9983876	0.0287553	0.5034965	1.4835681
STRLINCAR	18878	0.9975962	0.0322332	0.4697802	1.4835681

Differences between actual and imputed prices (in percent):

Variable	N	Mean	Std Dev	Minimum	Maximum
DLINCELL	16123	0.0112153	0.0356245	0	0.9861111
DLINCAR	17636	0.0120494	0.0393572	0	1.0989305
D2LINCELL	10134	0.0160790	0.0465267	0	1.1087869
D2LINCAR	11104	0.0173358	0.0564909	0	2.1978610
D3LINCELL	4939	0.0272895	0.0756754	0	1.3578140
D3LINCAR	5523	0.0282794	0.0985733	0	3.2967914

(B) Imports

Short-term relative between imputed and non-imputed price:

Variable	N	Mean	Std Dev	Minimum	Maximum
STRTRUE	21707	0.9997204	0.0558327	0.2290744	6.0085437
STRLINCELL	15872	0.9982729	0.0290135	0.4766223	1.5384615
STRLINCAR	18428	0.9970780	0.0318351	0.4611679	1.5384615

Differences between actual and imputed prices (in percent):

Variable	N	Mean	Std Dev	Minimum	Maximum
DLINCELL	15722	0.0125360	0.0365089	0	1.1431293
DLINCAR	17190	0.0134164	0.0555605	0	5.0085520
D2LINCELL	10332	0.0180936	0.0539739	0	1.9998297
D2LINCAR	11245	0.0189168	0.0593021	0	2.3368150
D3LINCELL	4793	0.0274864	0.0802594	0	2.9997446
D3LINCAR	5307	0.0272394	0.0901576	0	3.5052224

Note: These calculations are done over observations in the artificial dataset that are not imputed, but have their lagged value imputed.

3) *Linear interpolation results in less fluctuation of prices than the true series:*
In both the theory and empirical results, linear interpolation results in much smoother series. Indeed, the month-to-month fluctuation of these prices is even less than the true prices. This technique requires, however, that past information be stored until a new price quote is available, and then that the official price index be revised. If there is a limit on how many months of past information is stored, then hybrid techniques should be considered.

4) *Combining either carry-forward or cell-mean with linear interpolation gives similar results:*
Two hybrid techniques were considered, the first of which carried forward the prices, and the second of which used short term cell mean imputation, until the linear interpolation could begin. In both cases, linear interpolation was done over the previous three months (or less). The two hybrid techniques gave remarkably similar results.

5) *Computing cell-means for the same country of origin/destination and nearest product group gives nearly identical results to just using the nearest product group:*
Rather than just using Enduse categories for the cell mean imputation, we have examined whether import prices should also be imputed using price data from the same countries of origin, and export prices from the same country of destination. We expect that having the same exchange rate changes would lead to more consistent movements in prices than just being in the same Enduse category. However, in practice we find that this extra information does not improve the accuracy of the imputation method, at least not at the aggregate level of total exports or imports.

References

Alterman, W.F., W.E. Diewert and R.C. Feenstra (1999), *International Trade Price Indexes and Seasonal Commodities*, U.S. Department of Labor, Bureau of Labor Statistics, Washington, D.C.

Armknecht, P. A. and F. Maitland-Smith (1999) "Price Imputation and Other Techniques for Dealing with Missing Observations, Seasonality and Quality Changes in Prices Indices," IMF Working Paper 99/78, Statistics Department, International Monetary Fund, Washington, D.C.

Bryan, M.F. and S.G. Cecchetti (1993), "The Consumer Price Index as a Measure of Inflation", *Federal Reserve Bank of Cleveland Economic Review*, 15-24.

Bryan, M.F. and S.G. Cecchetti (1994), "Measuring Core Inflation", pp. 195-215 in G. Mankiw (ed.), *Monetary Policy*, Chicago: The University of Chicago Press.

Cecchetti, S.G. (1997), "Measuring Inflation for Central Bankers", *Federal Reserve Bank of St. Louis Review* 79:2, 143-155.

Clements, D.W. and H.Y. Izan (1987), "The Measurement of Inflation: a Stochastic Approach", *Journal of Business and Economic Statistics* 5, 339-350.

Diewert, W.E. (1995), "On the Stochastic Approach to Index Numbers", Discussion Paper 95-31, Department of Economics, University of British Columbia, Vancouver, Canada.

Diewert, W.E. (1997), "Commentary", *Federal Reserve Bank of St. Louis Review* 79:2, 127-137.

Diewert, W.E. (1998), "High Inflation, Seasonal Commodities and Annual Index Numbers", *Macroeconomic Dynamics* 2, 456-471.

Diewert, W.E. (1999), "Index Number Approaches to Seasonal Adjustment", *Macroeconomic Dynamics* 3, 48-68.

Selvanathan, E.A. and D.S. Prasada Rao (1994), *Index Numbers: a Stochastic Approach*, Michigan: University of Michigan Press.

Wynne, M.A. (1997), "Commentary", *Federal Reserve Bank of St. Louis Review* 79:2, 161-167.

Wynne, M.A. (1999), "Core Inflation: a Review of some Conceptual Issues", Research Department Working Paper 99-03, Federal Reserve Bank of Dallas, Dallas Texas.

Appendix

Proof of Proposition 1:

From (20) and (23) with $w_\beta = w_\gamma$, we readily obtain,

(A1) $\quad \Delta^*(t-1,t) \equiv [P^*(0,t)/ P_\alpha(0,t) - P^*(0,t-1)/ P_\alpha(0,t-1)]$

$\qquad = w_\beta [P_\beta(0,t)/P_\alpha(0,t) - P_\gamma(0,t-1)/P_\alpha(0,t-1)]/ (w_\alpha + w_\beta), \text{ for t odd}$

$\qquad = w_\beta [P_\gamma(0,t)/P_\alpha(0,t) - P_\beta(0,t-1)/P_\alpha(0,t-1)]/ (w_\alpha + w_\beta), \text{ for t even.}$

Condition (25) ensures that $P_\beta(0,t)/P_\alpha(0,t) \geq 1 \geq P_\gamma(0,t-1)/P_\alpha(0,t-1)$, for all t. Then we see from (A1) that $\Delta^*(t-1,t) \geq 0$ for t odd, and $\Delta^*(t-1,t) \leq 0$ for t even, so that part (a) follows directly.

Summing (A1) over two periods, we obtain ,

(A2) $\quad \Delta^*(t-2,t) = \Delta^*(t-2,t-1) + \Delta^*(t-1,t)$

$\qquad = w_\beta [P_\beta(0,t)/P_\alpha(0,t) - P_\beta(0,t-2)/P_\alpha(0,t-2)]/ (w_\alpha + w_\beta), \quad \text{for t odd}$

$\qquad = w_\beta [P_\gamma(0,t)/P_\alpha(0,t) - P_\gamma(0,t-2)/P_\alpha(0,t-2)]/ (w_\alpha + w_\beta), \quad \text{for t even.}$

From the alternating sign pattern of $\Delta^*(t-1,t)$, it follows that,

(A3) $\quad \Delta^*(t-2,t) = \Delta^*(t-2,t-1) + \Delta^*(t-1,t)$

$\qquad\qquad = |\Delta^*(t-2,t-1)| - |\Delta^*(t-1,t)|, \text{ if t is even,}$

$\qquad\qquad = -|\Delta^*(t-2,t-1)| + |\Delta^*(t-1,t)|, \text{ if t is odd.}$

Therefore, regardless of the sign of $\Delta^*(t-2,t)$, we have,

(A4) $\quad |\Delta^*(t-2,t)| \leq \max \{ |\Delta^*(t-2,t-1)|, |\Delta^*(t-1,t)| \}$

which is part (b).

Proof of Proposition 2:

Choosing t as even, rewrite (32) for t-1 as,

(A5) $\quad P^{**}(0,t-1)/P_\alpha(0,t-1) - w_\gamma P_\gamma(0,t-2)/P_\alpha(0,t-2) = [w_\alpha + w_\beta P_\beta(0,t-1)/P_\alpha(0,t-1)]$

Substituting (A4) into (33), we obtain,

(A6) $P^{**}(0,t) = [P^{**}(0,t-1)/P_\alpha(0,t-1) - w_\gamma P_\gamma(0,t-2)/P_\alpha(0,t-2)]P_\alpha(0,t) + w_\gamma P_\gamma(0,t)$.

We therefore have,

(A7) $\Delta^{**}(t-1,t) \equiv [P^{**}(0,t)/P_\alpha(0,t) - P^{**}(0,t-1)/P_\alpha(0,t-1)]$

$= w_\gamma[P_\gamma(0,t)/P_\alpha(0,t) - P_\gamma(0,t-2)/P_\alpha(0,t-2)], \quad \text{from (A6)}$

$= \Delta^{*}(t-2,t) (w_\alpha + w_\beta), \text{ from (A2) with } w_\gamma = w_\beta.$

Our assumption that $w_\gamma = w_\beta > 0$ ensures that $(w_\alpha + w_\beta) < 1$, so taking the absolute value of (A7) we obtain Proposition 2. A similar proof applies for t odd, in which case the change in the index relative to the always available commodities becomes,

(A8) $\Delta^{**}(t-1,t) \equiv [P^{**}(0,t)/P_\alpha(0,t) - P^{**}(0,t-1)/P_\alpha(0,t-1)]$

$= w_\beta[P_\beta(0,t)/P_\alpha(0,t) - P_\beta(0,t-2)/P_\alpha(0,t-2)] .$

Proof of Proposition 3:

For t odd, we can compute from (42) to (46) that,

(A9) $\Delta^{****}(t-1,t) \equiv [P^{****}(0,t)/ P_\alpha(0,t) - P^{****}(0,t-1)/ P_\alpha(0,t-1)] .$

$= w_\beta[P_\beta(0,t)/P_\alpha(0,t) - P_\beta(0,t-2)/ P_\alpha(0,t-2)]/2$

$+ w_\gamma[P_\gamma(0,t+1)/P_\alpha(0,t+1) - P_\gamma(0,t-1)/ P_\alpha(0,t-1)]/2 .$

It follows directly from (A7)-(A8) that,

(A10) $\Delta^{****}(t-1,t) = [\Delta^{**}(t-1,t) + \Delta^{**}(t,t+1)]/2.$

Appendix to Imputation and Price Indexes:

Theory and Evidence from the International Price Program

By

Erwin Diewert,
University of British Columbia and NBER,

and

Robert Feenstra,
University of California, Davis, and NBER

Revised, June 2000

Appendix A: Calculations summarized at the One Digit Enduse Level

All calculations are done over observations in the artificial dataset that are not imputed, but have their lagged value imputed.

Table A1: Summary of Carry forward and Linear Interpolation

Variable	N	Mean	Std Dev	Minimum	Maximum
		ENDUSE1=Q0			
TIME	1582	4.8426043	3.7404577	2.0000000	27.0000000
STRTRUE	1852	0.9979966	0.0914904	0.3272171	2.0476190
STRCARRY	1582	0.9949178	0.1695491	0.3333333	2.8750000
STRLIN	1582	0.9943733	0.0431000	0.6000000	1.3009709
DIFCARRY	1429	0.0707498	0.1332611	0	2.0000000
DIFLIN	1429	0.0349059	0.0723575	0	0.8730159
DIF2CARRY	813	0.0763454	0.1304689	0	0.9677419
DIF2LIN	813	0.0468441	0.0864990	0	0.8152174
DIF3CARRY	498	0.0827904	0.1510523	0	1.1982759
DIF3LIN	498	0.0614161	0.1348614	0	1.5155280
		ENDUSE1=Q1			
TIME	4951	4.2904464	3.2856080	2.0000000	31.0000000
STRTRUE	5642	0.9998524	0.0489944	0.6363636	3.0000000
STRCARRY	4951	0.9956972	0.1255152	0.3333333	6.0000000
STRLIN	4951	0.9974976	0.0275145	0.5034965	1.4835681
DIFCARRY	4594	0.0335765	0.0952780	0	2.0000000
DIFLIN	4594	0.0139504	0.0385242	0	0.9861111
DIF2CARRY	2824	0.0316666	0.0832106	0	1.6097272
DIF2LIN	2824	0.0184297	0.0431186	0	0.8098627
DIF3CARRY	1449	0.0389857	0.0956528	0	1.6097272
DIF3LIN	1449	0.0249082	0.0544257	0	0.9698356
		ENDUSE1=Q2			
TIME	8302	4.0446880	2.9425782	2.0000000	29.0000000
STRTRUE	9611	0.9997306	0.0335680	0.4791214	1.9318885
STRCARRY	8302	0.9989506	0.0700836	0.2280000	2.5325713
STRLIN	8302	0.9985971	0.0207632	0.6453840	1.3178458
DIFCARRY	7802	0.0146706	0.0765564	0	3.2967914
DIFLIN	7802	0.0062771	0.0281399	0	0.6092308
DIF2CARRY	5022	0.0136654	0.0782518	0	3.2967914
DIF2LIN	5022	0.0082482	0.0336968	0	1.0989305
DIF3CARRY	2325	0.0191664	0.1007765	0	3.2967914
DIF3LIN	2325	0.0124385	0.0507853	0	1.6483957
		ENDUSE1=Q3			
TIME	1259	4.1477363	3.0694817	2.0000000	28.0000000
STRTRUE	1451	1.0002257	0.0156591	0.7299592	1.1713918
STRCARRY	1259	1.0028396	0.0392825	0.6758850	1.5589744
STRLIN	1259	1.0000837	0.0100613	0.8902237	1.0889248
DIFCARRY	1187	0.0081596	0.0295958	0	0.4795417
DIFLIN	1187	0.0037114	0.0124451	0	0.1800272
DIF2CARRY	756	0.0072303	0.0308271	0	0.4795417
DIF2LIN	756	0.0047866	0.0145306	0	0.2397709
DIF3CARRY	381	0.0088134	0.0319202	0	0.3585526
DIF3LIN	381	0.0060063	0.0139541	0	0.0979544
		ENDUSE1=Q4			

TIME	2784	4.2018678	3.1797594	2.0000000	31.0000000
STRTRUE	3308	0.9999279	0.0257857	0.5832432	1.3617886
STRCARRY	2784	1.0013367	0.0520595	0.4970696	1.6666667
STRLIN	2784	0.9999115	0.0161961	0.7367702	1.1431452
DIFCARRY	2624	0.0116511	0.0520261	0	1.0117907
DIFLIN	2624	0.0056021	0.0233469	0	0.3386308
DIF2CARRY	1689	0.0108898	0.0506965	0	1.0117907
DIF2LIN	1689	0.0074810	0.0256037	0	0.3173611
DIF3CARRY	870	0.0121235	0.0574414	0	1.0117907
DIF3LIN	870	0.0084229	0.0237265	0	0.1856469

ENDUSE1=R0

TIME	1413	4.4331210	3.2681104	2.0000000	27.0000000
STRTRUE	1530	1.0043276	0.0932048	0.5430050	3.4000000
STRCARRY	1413	1.0062538	0.1499773	0.2694444	2.7076923
STRLIN	1413	0.9979063	0.0378545	0.5295090	1.2401961
DIFCARRY	1278	0.0535630	0.1087410	0	1.2888889
DIFLIN	1278	0.0272681	0.0784005	0	2.2000000
DIF2CARRY	851	0.0467411	0.1021676	0	1.0600000
DIF2LIN	851	0.0328124	0.0895517	0	2.0000001
DIF3CARRY	398	0.0496713	0.1078141	0	0.8571429
DIF3LIN	398	0.0339190	0.0686334	0	0.7142857

ENDUSE1=R1

TIME	3465	4.3012987	3.1228431	2.0000000	27.0000000
STRTRUE	3936	0.9983246	0.0483789	0.4320000	1.9191911
STRCARRY	3465	0.9919945	0.0946112	0.3378380	2.0615863
STRLIN	3465	0.9972982	0.0262135	0.7356322	1.3051775
DIFCARRY	3158	0.0352574	0.0755320	0	1.0738581
DIFLIN	3158	0.0169408	0.0354302	0	0.4704445
DIF2CARRY	1967	0.0350553	0.0750567	0	1.0738581
DIF2LIN	1967	0.0218910	0.0423956	0	0.5416667
DIF3CARRY	1013	0.0374826	0.0768643	0	0.6785502
DIF3LIN	1013	0.0254756	0.0449708	0	0.4779218

ENDUSE1=R2

TIME	6562	4.0356599	2.8758717	2.0000000	33.0000000
STRTRUE	7733	0.9998644	0.0694854	0.2290744	6.0085437
STRCARRY	6562	0.9956076	0.0984188	0.2219646	3.3333333
STRLIN	6562	0.9976863	0.0275983	0.5094340	1.5384615
DIFCARRY	6215	0.0266615	0.1217863	0	5.0085687
DIFLIN	6215	0.0113784	0.0723162	0	5.0085499
DIF2CARRY	4036	0.0244315	0.1091703	0	3.5052224
DIF2LIN	4036	0.0156330	0.0535321	0	1.9259259
DIF3CARRY	1792	0.0287046	0.1223993	0	3.5052224
DIF3LIN	1792	0.0196938	0.0537090	0	0.7908163

ENDUSE1=R3

TIME	1812	3.8940397	2.7855087	2.0000000	26.0000000
STRTRUE	2131	0.9992863	0.0233400	0.7000000	1.2647777
STRCARRY	1812	0.9978240	0.0502992	0.4380228	1.5394642
STRLIN	1812	0.9990185	0.0154718	0.7957999	1.2124323
DIFCARRY	1701	0.0154366	0.0506706	0	1.2829861
DIFLIN	1701	0.0069995	0.0187786	0	0.2565972
DIF2CARRY	1063	0.0147397	0.0565511	0	1.2829861
DIF2LIN	1063	0.0097363	0.0260721	0	0.5131944
DIF3CARRY	439	0.0196139	0.0517781	0	0.5074106
DIF3LIN	439	0.0136510	0.0284558	0	0.2247909

ENDUSE1=R4

TIME	5176	4.4350850	3.2015150	2.0000000	28.0000000
STRTRUE	6379	0.9994473	0.0322610	0.3449163	2.5000000
STRCARRY	5176	0.9972009	0.0726254	0.3750000	4.1176484
STRLIN	5176	0.9988871	0.0148218	0.5454545	1.2055376
DIFCARRY	4838	0.0141074	0.0527317	0	1.6666667
DIFLIN	4838	0.0064520	0.0317945	0	1.2333333
DIF2CARRY	3328	0.0129019	0.0445197	0	0.8454546
DIF2LIN	3328	0.0079998	0.0304330	0	0.9666667
DIF3CARRY	1665	0.0160789	0.0489429	0	0.7571429
DIF3LIN	1665	0.0106908	0.0282747	0	0.4166667

Table A2: Summary of Linear and Hybrid Interpolation

Variable	N	Mean	Std Dev	Minimum	Maximum
		ENDUSE1=Q0			
TIME	1582	4.8426043	3.7404577	2.0000000	27.0000000
STRTRUE	1852	0.9979966	0.0914904	0.3272171	2.0476190
STRLIN	1582	0.9943733	0.0431000	0.6000000	1.3009709
STRLINCAR	1582	0.9922815	0.0576276	0.6000000	1.3009709
DIFLIN	1429	0.0349059	0.0723575	0	0.8730159
DLINCAR	1429	0.0390300	0.0727753	0	0.8730159
DIF2LIN	813	0.0468441	0.0864990	0	0.8152174
D2LINCAR	813	0.0582669	0.0970004	0	0.8315412
DIF3LIN	498	0.0614161	0.1348614	0	1.5155280
D3LINCAR	498	0.0827904	0.1510523	0	1.1982759
		ENDUSE1=Q1			
TIME	4951	4.2904464	3.2856080	2.0000000	31.0000000
STRTRUE	5642	0.9998524	0.0489944	0.6363636	3.0000000
STRLIN	4951	0.9974976	0.0275145	0.5034965	1.4835681
STRLINCAR	4951	0.9959757	0.0361748	0.5034965	1.4835681
DIFLIN	4594	0.0139504	0.0385242	0	0.9861111
DLINCAR	4594	0.0161120	0.0419056	0	0.9861111
DIF2LIN	2824	0.0184297	0.0431186	0	0.8098627
D2LINCAR	2824	0.0238082	0.0571442	0	1.2364571
DIF3LIN	1449	0.0249082	0.0544257	0	0.9698356
D3LINCAR	1449	0.0389857	0.0956528	0	1.6097272
		ENDUSE1=Q2			
TIME	8302	4.0446880	2.9425782	2.0000000	29.0000000
STRTRUE	9611	0.9997306	0.0335680	0.4791214	1.9318885
STRLIN	8302	0.9985971	0.0207632	0.6453840	1.3178458
STRLINCAR	8302	0.9983514	0.0278322	0.4697802	1.3178458
DIFLIN	7802	0.0062771	0.0281399	0	0.6092308
DLINCAR	7802	0.0076828	0.0326604	0	1.0989305
DIF2LIN	5022	0.0082482	0.0336968	0	1.0989305
D2LINCAR	5022	0.0113300	0.0531150	0	2.1978610
DIF3LIN	2325	0.0124385	0.0507853	0	1.6483957
D3LINCAR	2325	0.0191664	0.1007765	0	3.2967914
		ENDUSE1=Q3			

TIME	1259	4.1477363	3.0694817	2.0000000	28.0000000
STRTRUE	1451	1.0002257	0.0156591	0.7299592	1.1713918
STRLIN	1259	1.0000837	0.0100613	0.8902237	1.0889248
STRLINCAR	1259	1.0005957	0.0135063	0.8621825	1.1357410
DIFLIN	1187	0.0037114	0.0124451	0	0.1800272
DLINCAR	1187	0.0044735	0.0140487	0	0.1800272
DIF2LIN	756	0.0047866	0.0145306	0	0.2397709
D2LINCAR	756	0.0063107	0.0213526	0	0.3196945
DIF3LIN	381	0.0060063	0.0139541	0	0.0979544
D3LINCAR	381	0.0088134	0.0319202	0	0.3585526

ENDUSE1=Q4

TIME	2784	4.2018678	3.1797594	2.0000000	31.0000000
STRTRUE	3308	0.9999279	0.0257857	0.5832432	1.3617886
STRLIN	2784	0.9999115	0.0161961	0.7367702	1.1431452
STRLINCAR	2784	0.9998895	0.0202101	0.7367702	1.1538462
DIFLIN	2624	0.0056021	0.0233469	0	0.3386308
DLINCAR	2624	0.0066535	0.0256295	0	0.3691932
DIF2LIN	1689	0.0074810	0.0256037	0	0.3173611
D2LINCAR	1689	0.0096042	0.0361812	0	0.6745271
DIF3LIN	870	0.0084229	0.0237265	0	0.1856469
D3LINCAR	870	0.0121235	0.0574414	0	1.0117907

ENDUSE1=R0

TIME	1413	4.4331210	3.2681104	2.0000000	27.0000000
STRTRUE	1530	1.0043276	0.0932048	0.5430050	3.4000000
STRLIN	1413	0.9979063	0.0378545	0.5295090	1.2401961
STRLINCAR	1413	0.9977286	0.0491242	0.5252707	1.2661871
DIFLIN	1278	0.0272681	0.0784005	0	2.2000000
DLINCAR	1278	0.0296112	0.0711173	0	1.7333334
DIF2LIN	851	0.0328124	0.0895517	0	2.0000001
D2LINCAR	851	0.0369317	0.0804525	0	1.0666669
DIF3LIN	398	0.0339190	0.0686334	0	0.7142857
D3LINCAR	398	0.0496713	0.1078141	0	0.8571429

ENDUSE1=R1

TIME	3465	4.3012987	3.1228431	2.0000000	27.0000000
STRTRUE	3936	0.9983246	0.0483789	0.4320000	1.9191911
STRLIN	3465	0.9972982	0.0262135	0.7356322	1.3051775
STRLINCAR	3465	0.9953116	0.0344755	0.6048389	1.3051775
DIFLIN	3158	0.0169408	0.0354302	0	0.4704445
DLINCAR	3158	0.0188087	0.0372028	0	0.4704445
DIF2LIN	1967	0.0218910	0.0423956	0	0.5416667
D2LINCAR	1967	0.0273439	0.0533132	0	0.7159054
DIF3LIN	1013	0.0254756	0.0449708	0	0.4779218
D3LINCAR	1013	0.0374826	0.0768643	0	0.6785502

ENDUSE1=R2

TIME	6562	4.0356599	2.8758717	2.0000000	33.0000000
STRTRUE	7733	0.9998644	0.0694854	0.2290744	6.0085437
STRLIN	6562	0.9976863	0.0275983	0.5094340	1.5384615
STRLINCAR	6562	0.9965249	0.0357833	0.4611679	1.5384615
DIFLIN	6215	0.0113784	0.0723162	0	5.0085499
DLINCAR	6215	0.0133425	0.0758595	0	5.0085520
DIF2LIN	4036	0.0156330	0.0535321	0	1.9259259
D2LINCAR	4036	0.0197693	0.0741107	0	2.3368150
DIF3LIN	1792	0.0196938	0.0537090	0	0.7908163
D3LINCAR	1792	0.0287046	0.1223993	0	3.5052224

ENDUSE1=R3

TIME	1812	3.8940397	2.7855087	2.0000000	26.0000000
STRTRUE	2131	0.9992863	0.0233400	0.7000000	1.2647777
STRLIN	1812	0.9990185	0.0154718	0.7957999	1.2124323
STRLINCAR	1812	0.9986925	0.0194168	0.7004459	1.2124323
DIFLIN	1701	0.0069995	0.0187786	0	0.2565972
DLINCAR	1701	0.0081362	0.0221404	0	0.4276620
DIF2LIN	1063	0.0097363	0.0260721	0	0.5131944
D2LINCAR	1063	0.0125322	0.0387303	0	0.8553241
DIF3LIN	439	0.0136510	0.0284558	0	0.2247909
D3LINCAR	439	0.0196139	0.0517781	0	0.5074106

ENDUSE1=R4

TIME	5176	4.4350850	3.2015150	2.0000000	28.0000000
STRTRUE	6379	0.9994473	0.0322610	0.3449163	2.5000000
STRLIN	5176	0.9988871	0.0148218	0.5454545	1.2055376
STRLINCAR	5176	0.9982188	0.0198642	0.5454545	1.3375797
DIFLIN	4838	0.0064520	0.0317945	0	1.2333333
DLINCAR	4838	0.0075700	0.0321552	0	1.1444444
DIF2LIN	3328	0.0079998	0.0304330	0	0.9666667
D2LINCAR	3328	0.0103350	0.0346329	0	0.7888889
DIF3LIN	1665	0.0106908	0.0282747	0	0.4166667
D3LINCAR	1665	0.0160789	0.0489429	0	0.7571429

Table A3: Summary of Hybrid and Cell Mean Interpolation

Variable	N	Mean	Std Dev	Minimum	Maximum
		ENDUSE1=Q0			
TIME	1582	4.8426043	3.7404577	2.0000000	27.0000000
STRTRUE	1852	0.9979966	0.0914904	0.3272171	2.0476190
STRCELL	1331	0.9998152	0.1329827	0.3926315	2.1160876
STRLINCAR	1582	0.9922815	0.0576276	0.6000000	1.3009709
DIFCELL	1331	0.0645312	0.1190780	0	1.5921214
DLINCAR	1429	0.0390300	0.0727753	0	0.8730159
DIF2CELL	752	0.0655651	0.1297158	0	1.5469176
D2LINCAR	813	0.0582669	0.0970004	0	0.8315412
DIF3CELL	466	0.0726033	0.1521785	0	1.9076840
D3LINCAR	498	0.0827904	0.1510523	0	1.1982759
		ENDUSE1=Q1			
TIME	4951	4.2904464	3.2856080	2.0000000	31.0000000
STRTRUE	5642	0.9998524	0.0489944	0.6363636	3.0000000
STRCELL	4384	1.0014346	0.0851738	0.2926829	2.2299381
STRLINCAR	4951	0.9959757	0.0361748	0.5034965	1.4835681
DIFCELL	4384	0.0326232	0.1029829	0	2.4166667
DLINCAR	4594	0.0161120	0.0419056	0	0.9861111
DIF2CELL	2683	0.0285953	0.0851506	0	2.4166667
D2LINCAR	2824	0.0238082	0.0571442	0	1.2364571
DIF3CELL	1381	0.0338503	0.1003722	0	2.4166667
D3LINCAR	1449	0.0389857	0.0956528	0	1.6097272
		ENDUSE1=Q2			

TIME	8302	4.0446880	2.9425782	2.0000000	29.0000000
STRTRUE	9611	0.9997306	0.0335680	0.4791214	1.9318885
STRCELL	7617	1.0013616	0.0926208	0.3296220	6.8796068
STRLINCAR	8302	0.9983514	0.0278322	0.4697802	1.3178458
DIFCELL	7617	0.0154992	0.0619661	0	2.0337778
DLINCAR	7802	0.0076828	0.0326604	0	1.0989305
DIF2CELL	4844	0.0135335	0.0553870	0	1.8768984
D2LINCAR	5022	0.0113300	0.0531150	0	2.1978610
DIF3CELL	2231	0.0175443	0.0623078	0	1.0008230
D3LINCAR	2325	0.0191664	0.1007765	0	3.2967914

ENDUSE1=Q3

TIME	1259	4.1477363	3.0694817	2.0000000	28.0000000
STRTRUE	1451	1.0002257	0.0156591	0.7299592	1.1713918
STRCELL	1169	1.0001853	0.0299938	0.6632121	1.3965411
STRLINCAR	1259	1.0005957	0.0135063	0.8621825	1.1357410
DIFCELL	1169	0.0076029	0.0260350	0	0.5078133
DLINCAR	1187	0.0044735	0.0140487	0	0.1800272
DIF2CELL	742	0.0070823	0.0270598	0	0.5078133
D2LINCAR	756	0.0063107	0.0213526	0	0.3196945
DIF3CELL	371	0.0087481	0.0240834	0	0.2839452
D3LINCAR	381	0.0088134	0.0319202	0	0.3585526

ENDUSE1=Q4

TIME	2784	4.2018678	3.1797594	2.0000000	31.0000000
STRTRUE	3308	0.9999279	0.0257857	0.5832432	1.3617886
STRCELL	2556	1.0025433	0.1046647	0.5832432	5.6151035
STRLINCAR	2784	0.9998895	0.0202101	0.7367702	1.1538462
DIFCELL	2556	0.0132494	0.0494703	0	0.8219089
DLINCAR	2624	0.0066535	0.0256295	0	0.3691932
DIF2CELL	1643	0.0117912	0.0412122	0	0.5665821
D2LINCAR	1689	0.0096042	0.0361812	0	0.6745271
DIF3CELL	848	0.0141020	0.0408778	0	0.3705618
D3LINCAR	870	0.0121235	0.0574414	0	1.0117907

ENDUSE1=R0

TIME	1413	4.4331210	3.2681104	2.0000000	27.0000000
STRTRUE	1530	1.0043276	0.0932048	0.5430050	3.4000000
STRCELL	1202	1.0039291	0.1108324	0.3708447	2.0000000
STRLINCAR	1413	0.9977286	0.0491242	0.5252707	1.2661871
DIFCELL	1202	0.0446586	0.0974266	0	1.1977481
DLINCAR	1278	0.0296112	0.0711173	0	1.7333334
DIF2CELL	805	0.0407679	0.0993594	0	1.2940989
D2LINCAR	851	0.0369317	0.0804525	0	1.0666669
DIF3CELL	375	0.0428251	0.0841829	0	0.7394237
D3LINCAR	398	0.0496713	0.1078141	0	0.8571429

ENDUSE1=R1

TIME	3465	4.3012987	3.1228431	2.0000000	27.0000000
STRTRUE	3936	0.9983246	0.0483789	0.4320000	1.9191911
STRCELL	3013	1.0034513	0.0880458	0.5507463	1.8573643
STRLINCAR	3465	0.9953116	0.0344755	0.6048389	1.3051775
DIFCELL	3013	0.0332836	0.0615568	0	0.8157182
DLINCAR	3158	0.0188087	0.0372028	0	0.4704445
DIF2CELL	1875	0.0317941	0.0581629	0	0.5656039
D2LINCAR	1967	0.0273439	0.0533132	0	0.7159054
DIF3CELL	976	0.0326728	0.0582158	0	0.6054766
D3LINCAR	1013	0.0374826	0.0768643	0	0.6785502

ENDUSE1=R2

TIME	6562	4.0356599	2.8758717	2.0000000	33.0000000
STRTRUE	7733	0.9998644	0.0694854	0.2290744	6.0085437
STRCELL	6053	1.0040604	0.1049234	0.2302684	3.1609195
STRLINCAR	6562	0.9965249	0.0357833	0.4611679	1.5384615
DIFCELL	6053	0.0280084	0.0955613	0	2.9319156
DLINCAR	6215	0.0133425	0.0758595	0	5.0085520
DIF2CELL	3887	0.0255012	0.0993012	0	2.9319156
D2LINCAR	4036	0.0197693	0.0741107	0	2.3368150
DIF3CELL	1711	0.0315992	0.1119094	0	2.9319156
D3LINCAR	1792	0.0287046	0.1223993	0	3.5052224

ENDUSE1=R3

TIME	1812	3.8940397	2.7855087	2.0000000	26.0000000
STRTRUE	2131	0.9992863	0.0233400	0.7000000	1.2647777
STRCELL	1654	0.9989410	0.0505366	0.4380228	1.5394431
STRLINCAR	1812	0.9986925	0.0194168	0.7004459	1.2124323
DIFCELL	1654	0.0152213	0.0495900	0	1.2829861
DLINCAR	1701	0.0081362	0.0221404	0	0.4276620
DIF2CELL	1031	0.0141403	0.0546510	0	1.2829861
D2LINCAR	1063	0.0125322	0.0387303	0	0.8553241
DIF3CELL	426	0.0193361	0.0492917	0	0.5598410
D3LINCAR	439	0.0196139	0.0517781	0	0.5074106

ENDUSE1=R4

TIME	5176	4.4350850	3.2015150	2.0000000	28.0000000
STRTRUE	6379	0.9994473	0.0322610	0.3449163	2.5000000
STRCELL	4675	0.9999431	0.0529228	0.3737137	2.2466758
STRLINCAR	5176	0.9982188	0.0198642	0.5454545	1.3375797
DIFCELL	4675	0.0157186	0.0563854	0	1.6758455
DLINCAR	4838	0.0075700	0.0321552	0	1.1444444
DIF2CELL	3187	0.0143431	0.0495822	0	1.3344772
D2LINCAR	3328	0.0103350	0.0346329	0	0.7888889
DIF3CELL	1594	0.0170467	0.0539397	0	1.3344772
D3LINCAR	1665	0.0160789	0.0489429	0	0.7571429

Table A4: Summary of Two Hybrid Techniques

Variable	N	Mean	Std Dev	Minimum	Maximum

ENDUSE1=Q0

TIME	1205	3.8713693	2.9016352	2.0000000	27.0000000
STRTRUE	1842	0.9985856	0.0911652	0.3272171	2.0476190
STRLINCELL	1205	0.9926552	0.0545811	0.6000000	1.3009709
STRLINCAR	1205	0.9930393	0.0564237	0.6000000	1.3009709
DLINCELL	1205	0.0354888	0.0671234	0	0.8730159
DLINCAR	1205	0.0355229	0.0674264	0	0.8730159
D2LINCELL	702	0.0517804	0.0959472	0	0.9583673
D2LINCAR	702	0.0530525	0.0921017	0	0.8315412
D3LINCELL	437	0.0740230	0.1563516	0	1.9076840
D3LINCAR	437	0.0793541	0.1501130	0	1.1982759

ENDUSE1=Q1

TIME	4131	3.6548051	2.5113665	2.0000000	29.0000000
STRTRUE	5616	0.9998155	0.0491116	0.6363636	3.0000000
STRLINCELL	4131	0.9978198	0.0337674	0.5034965	1.4835681
STRLINCAR	4131	0.9969140	0.0346091	0.5034965	1.4835681
DLINCELL	4131	0.0152940	0.0437332	0	0.9861111
DLINCAR	4131	0.0152400	0.0414391	0	0.9861111
D2LINCELL	2569	0.0217348	0.0596800	0	1.6111111
D2LINCAR	2569	0.0213714	0.0521049	0	1.2364571
D3LINCELL	1308	0.0332154	0.1021958	0	2.4166667
D3LINCAR	1308	0.0350617	0.0897575	0	1.6097272

ENDUSE1=Q2

TIME	7184	3.5494154	2.2880564	2.0000000	29.0000000
STRTRUE	9593	0.9997301	0.0335995	0.4791214	1.9318885
STRLINCELL	7184	0.9988495	0.0236116	0.6103305	1.3983686
STRLINCAR	7184	0.9987393	0.0232930	0.6102610	1.3178458
DLINCELL	7184	0.0069871	0.0277936	0	0.6384565
DLINCAR	7184	0.0068434	0.0280978	0	0.6386431
D2LINCELL	4661	0.0102864	0.0390106	0	1.2470844
D2LINCAR	4661	0.0097537	0.0400549	0	1.2474527
D3LINCELL	2123	0.0172978	0.0628442	0	1.0008230
D3LINCAR	2123	0.0149747	0.0657546	0	1.2500000

ENDUSE1=Q3

TIME	1096	3.7627737	2.8051357	2.0000000	28.0000000
STRTRUE	1449	1.0002260	0.0156699	0.7299592	1.1713918
STRLINCELL	1096	1.0001296	0.0118352	0.8726495	1.1045432
STRLINCAR	1096	1.0003954	0.0123480	0.8621825	1.1357410
DLINCELL	1096	0.0043716	0.0131806	0	0.1800272
DLINCAR	1096	0.0043067	0.0136457	0	0.1800272
D2LINCELL	706	0.0061196	0.0178292	0	0.2918709
D2LINCAR	706	0.0059525	0.0198745	0	0.3196945
D3LINCELL	349	0.0089548	0.0246903	0	0.2839452
D3LINCAR	349	0.0085025	0.0286370	0	0.3585526

ENDUSE1=Q4

TIME	2430	3.7695473	2.7738224	2.0000000	29.0000000
STRTRUE	3291	0.9999276	0.0258523	0.5832432	1.3617886
STRLINCELL	2430	0.9999600	0.0189773	0.7367702	1.1431452
STRLINCAR	2430	0.9998618	0.0198208	0.7367702	1.1431452
DLINCELL	2430	0.0064336	0.0228277	0	0.3319444
DLINCAR	2430	0.0062861	0.0250296	0	0.3691932
D2LINCELL	1587	0.0094542	0.0287930	0	0.3418803
D2LINCAR	1587	0.0090739	0.0363295	0	0.6745271
D3LINCELL	817	0.0136226	0.0406970	0	0.3705618
D3LINCAR	817	0.0116980	0.0584845	0	1.0117907

ENDUSE1=R0

TIME	1124	3.5498221	2.1556135	2.0000000	21.0000000
STRTRUE	1523	1.0044221	0.0934059	0.5430050	3.4000000
STRLINCELL	1124	0.9984703	0.0431729	0.5295090	1.2401961
STRLINCAR	1124	0.9985415	0.0444574	0.5295090	1.2661871
DLINCELL	1124	0.0250578	0.0458115	0	0.4166667
DLINCAR	1124	0.0253423	0.0482454	0	0.4296296
D2LINCELL	762	0.0320523	0.0600956	0	0.5786269
D2LINCAR	762	0.0317260	0.0653039	0	0.6733333
D3LINCELL	353	0.0411780	0.0837808	0	0.7394237
D3LINCAR	353	0.0415209	0.0960728	0	0.8571429

ENDUSE1=R1

TIME	2821	3.6292095	2.3682409	2.0000000	21.0000000
STRTRUE	3917	0.9983165	0.0484960	0.4320000	1.9191911
STRLINCELL	2821	0.9981301	0.0311465	0.7356322	1.3051775
STRLINCAR	2821	0.9970343	0.0314984	0.7356322	1.3051775
DLINCELL	2821	0.0173123	0.0340001	0	0.4704445
DLINCAR	2821	0.0173418	0.0347843	0	0.4704445
D2LINCELL	1807	0.0236694	0.0434899	0	0.5416667
D2LINCAR	1807	0.0240660	0.0465864	0	0.5416667
D3LINCELL	942	0.0315938	0.0578769	0	0.6054766
D3LINCAR	942	0.0316922	0.0640690	0	0.6785502

ENDUSE1=R2

TIME	5725	3.5680349	2.2860877	2.0000000	33.0000000
STRTRUE	7719	0.9998407	0.0695373	0.2290744	6.0085437
STRLINCELL	5725	0.9976703	0.0329513	0.4729803	1.5384615
STRLINCAR	5725	0.9968464	0.0333897	0.4611679	1.5384615
DLINCELL	5725	0.0125507	0.0405171	0	0.9773052
DLINCAR	5725	0.0121678	0.0418388	0	1.1684075
D2LINCELL	3761	0.0196693	0.0700569	0	1.9546104
D2LINCAR	3761	0.0186333	0.0731312	0	2.3368150
D3LINCELL	1637	0.0306348	0.1113089	0	2.9319156
D3LINCAR	1637	0.0268448	0.1221300	0	3.5052224

ENDUSE1=R3

TIME	1583	3.4213519	2.0802421	2.0000000	23.0000000
STRTRUE	2128	0.9992853	0.0233565	0.7000000	1.2647777
STRLINCELL	1583	0.9987370	0.0198962	0.7004459	1.2124323
STRLINCAR	1583	0.9987559	0.0196821	0.7004459	1.2124323
DLINCELL	1583	0.0080434	0.0221095	0	0.4276620
DLINCAR	1583	0.0080239	0.0222434	0	0.4276620
D2LINCELL	999	0.0122673	0.0384390	0	0.8553241
D2LINCAR	999	0.0120969	0.0385898	0	0.8553241
D3LINCELL	409	0.0193786	0.0499313	0	0.5598410
D3LINCAR	409	0.0191072	0.0500997	0	0.5074106

ENDUSE1=R4

TIME	4384	3.8252737	2.4919748	2.0000000	26.0000000
STRTRUE	6337	0.9994576	0.0323881	0.3449163	2.5000000
STRLINCELL	4384	0.9990821	0.0179724	0.5454545	1.2269427
STRLINCAR	4384	0.9984820	0.0171546	0.5454545	1.1964286
DLINCELL	4384	0.0072529	0.0319666	0	1.1564735
DLINCAR	4384	0.0069067	0.0314661	0	1.1444444
D2LINCELL	3081	0.0104579	0.0366172	0	0.8896515
D2LINCAR	3081	0.0094628	0.0316656	0	0.7888889
D3LINCELL	1530	0.0167729	0.0542923	0	1.3344772
D3LINCAR	1530	0.0147633	0.0437723	0	0.4981550

Appendix B: One Digit Enduse Calculations – Using country of Origin/Destination

Table B1 can be compared with A3, and Table B2 can be compared with A4.

Table B1: Summary of Hybrid and Cell Mean Interpolation

Variable	N	Mean	Std Dev	Minimum	Maximum
ENDUSE1=Q0					
TIME	1582	4.8426043	3.7404577	2.0000000	27.0000000
STRTRUE	1852	0.9979966	0.0914904	0.3272171	2.0476190
STRCELL	1181	0.9977852	0.1304950	0.3985744	1.9352712
STRLINC	1582	0.9922815	0.0576276	0.6000000	1.3009709
DIFCELL	1181	0.0653753	0.1138434	0	1.4933779
DIFLINCAR	1429	0.0390300	0.0727753	0	0.8730159
DIF2CELL	691	0.0688210	0.1248084	0	1.4933779
D2LINCAR	813	0.0582669	0.0970004	0	0.8315412
DIF3CELL	432	0.0749512	0.1395148	0	1.2701575
D3LINCAR	498	0.0827904	0.1510523	0	1.1982759
ENDUSE1=Q1					
TIME	4951	4.2904464	3.2856080	2.0000000	31.0000000
STRTRUE	5642	0.9998524	0.0489944	0.6363636	3.0000000
STRCELL	4067	1.0018215	0.0951259	0.2926829	3.7960587
STRLINC	4951	0.9959757	0.0361748	0.5034965	1.4835681
DIFCELL	4067	0.0337571	0.0949557	0	2.4166667
DIFLINCAR	4594	0.0161120	0.0419056	0	0.9861111
DIF2CELL	2519	0.0293155	0.0696102	0	1.3578140
D2LINCAR	2824	0.0238082	0.0571442	0	1.2364571
DIF3CELL	1277	0.0348937	0.0767315	0	1.3578140
D3LINCAR	1449	0.0389857	0.0956528	0	1.6097272
ENDUSE1=Q2					
TIME	8302	4.0446880	2.9425782	2.0000000	29.0000000
STRTRUE	9611	0.9997306	0.0335680	0.4791214	1.9318885
STRCELL	7090	1.0016936	0.0937076	0.3706689	6.8796068
STRLINC	8302	0.9983514	0.0278322	0.4697802	1.3178458
DIFCELL	7090	0.0174331	0.0596768	0	1.6978255
DIFLINCAR	7802	0.0076828	0.0326604	0	1.0989305
DIF2CELL	4605	0.0159953	0.0572201	0	1.6529557
D2LINCAR	5022	0.0113300	0.0531150	0	2.1978610
DIF3CELL	2098	0.0205221	0.0661589	0	0.9955389
D3LINCAR	2325	0.0191664	0.1007765	0	3.2967914
ENDUSE1=Q3					
TIME	1259	4.1477363	3.0694817	2.0000000	28.0000000
STRTRUE	1451	1.0002257	0.0156591	0.7299592	1.1713918
STRCELL	1060	0.9999189	0.0302671	0.6772387	1.4537828
STRLINC	1259	1.0005957	0.0135063	0.8621825	1.1357410
DIFCELL	1060	0.0082751	0.0250245	0	0.4765842
DIFLINCAR	1187	0.0044735	0.0140487	0	0.1800272
DIF2CELL	684	0.0075015	0.0268495	0	0.4858251
D2LINCAR	756	0.0063107	0.0213526	0	0.3196945
DIF3CELL	336	0.0098889	0.0250145	0	0.2956747
D3LINCAR	381	0.0088134	0.0319202	0	0.3585526

ENDUSE1=Q4

TIME	2784	4.2018678	3.1797594	2.0000000	31.0000000
STRTRUE	3308	0.9999279	0.0257857	0.5832432	1.3617886
STRCELL	2348	1.0002902	0.0474986	0.5832432	1.5546794
STRLINC	2784	0.9998895	0.0202101	0.7367702	1.1538462
DIFCELL	2348	0.0127301	0.0447646	0	0.7127134
DIFLINCAR	2624	0.0066535	0.0256295	0	0.3691932
DIF2CELL	1538	0.0122769	0.0418017	0	0.6097781
D2LINCAR	1689	0.0096042	0.0361812	0	0.6745271
DIF3CELL	796	0.0144056	0.0449121	0	0.6097781
D3LINCAR	870	0.0121235	0.0574414	0	1.0117907

ENDUSE1=R0

TIME	1413	4.4331210	3.2681104	2.0000000	27.0000000
STRTRUE	1530	1.0043276	0.0932048	0.5430050	3.4000000
STRCELL	1085	1.0028296	0.1111144	0.3688633	2.0000000
STRLINC	1413	0.9977286	0.0491242	0.5252707	1.2661871
DIFCELL	1085	0.0467331	0.0999475	0	1.1829951
DIFLINCAR	1278	0.0296112	0.0711173	0	1.7333334
DIF2CELL	738	0.0422153	0.1001315	0	1.2940989
D2LINCAR	851	0.0369317	0.0804525	0	1.0666669
DIF3CELL	341	0.0424705	0.0809919	0	0.7065959
D3LINCAR	398	0.0496713	0.1078141	0	0.8571429

ENDUSE1=R1

TIME	3465	4.3012987	3.1228431	2.0000000	27.0000000
STRTRUE	3936	0.9983246	0.0483789	0.4320000	1.9191911
STRCELL	2761	1.0025935	0.0840698	0.5277925	1.8573643
STRLINC	3465	0.9953116	0.0344755	0.6048389	1.3051775
DIFCELL	2761	0.0335575	0.0620475	0	0.8946840
DIFLINCAR	3158	0.0188087	0.0372028	0	0.4704445
DIF2CELL	1763	0.0327616	0.0596562	0	0.5935764
D2LINCAR	1967	0.0273439	0.0533132	0	0.7159054
DIF3CELL	919	0.0347760	0.0593347	0	0.6302116
D3LINCAR	1013	0.0374826	0.0768643	0	0.6785502

ENDUSE1=R2

TIME	6562	4.0356599	2.8758717	2.0000000	33.0000000
STRTRUE	7733	0.9998644	0.0694854	0.2290744	6.0085437
STRCELL	5684	1.0014879	0.0994281	0.2328672	3.8014859
STRLINC	6562	0.9965249	0.0357833	0.4611679	1.5384615
DIFCELL	5684	0.0275460	0.0968671	0	2.9847505
DIFLINCAR	6215	0.0133425	0.0758595	0	5.0085520
DIF2CELL	3739	0.0257725	0.1004569	0	2.9928985
D2LINCAR	4036	0.0197693	0.0741107	0	2.3368150
DIF3CELL	1624	0.0316268	0.1110063	0	2.9997446
D3LINCAR	1792	0.0287046	0.1223993	0	3.5052224

ENDUSE1=R3

TIME	1812	3.8940397	2.7855087	2.0000000	26.0000000
STRTRUE	2131	0.9992863	0.0233400	0.7000000	1.2647777
STRCELL	1561	1.0013741	0.0505177	0.4380397	1.5394415
STRLINC	1812	0.9986925	0.0194168	0.7004459	1.2124323
DIFCELL	1561	0.0175614	0.0493846	0	1.2828981
DIFLINCAR	1701	0.0081362	0.0221404	0	0.4276620
DIF2CELL	983	0.0164783	0.0549816	0	1.2828981
D2LINCAR	1063	0.0125322	0.0387303	0	0.8553241
DIF3CELL	402	0.0226923	0.0484074	0	0.4370243
D3LINCAR	439	0.0196139	0.0517781	0	0.5074106

12

ENDUSE1=R4

TIME	5178	4.4333720	3.2020829	0	28.0000000
STRTRUE	6377	0.9994471	0.0322660	0.3449163	2.5000000
STRCELL	4325	1.0006284	0.0461530	0.3732686	1.8817753
STRLINC	5176	0.9982188	0.0198642	0.5454545	1.3375797
DIFCELL	4325	0.0142450	0.0512112	0	1.6790357
DIFLINCAR	4838	0.0075700	0.0321552	0	1.1444444
DIF2CELL	3044	0.0133833	0.0454624	0	1.3288201
D2LINCAR	3328	0.0103350	0.0346329	0	0.7888889
DIF3CELL	1507	0.0164676	0.0523135	0	1.3288201
D3LINCAR	1665	0.0160789	0.0489429	0	0.7571429

Table B2: Summary of Two Hybrid Techniques

Variable	N	Mean	Std Dev	Minimum	Maximum
		ENDUSE1=Q0			
TIME	1582	4.8426043	3.7404577	2.0000000	27.0000000
STRTRUE	1852	0.9979966	0.0914904	0.3272171	2.0476190
STRLINCELL	1243	0.9927726	0.0541436	0.6000000	1.3009709
STRLINCAR	1582	0.9922815	0.0576276	0.6000000	1.3009709
DIFLINCELL	1226	0.0356832	0.0664264	0	0.8730159
DIFLINCAR	1429	0.0390300	0.0727753	0	0.8730159
D2LINCELL	697	0.0517356	0.0918870	0	0.8941979
D2LINCAR	813	0.0582669	0.0970004	0	0.8315412
D3LINCELL	432	0.0749512	0.1395148	0	1.2701575
D3LINCAR	498	0.0827904	0.1510523	0	1.1982759
		ENDUSE1=Q1			
TIME	4951	4.2904464	3.2856080	2.0000000	31.0000000
STRTRUE	5642	0.9998524	0.0489944	0.6363636	3.0000000
STRLINCELL	4210	0.9978710	0.0331762	0.5034965	1.4835681
STRLINCAR	4951	0.9959757	0.0361748	0.5034965	1.4835681
DIFLINCELL	4158	0.0153407	0.0407516	0	0.9861111
DIFLINCAR	4594	0.0161120	0.0419056	0	0.9861111
D2LINCELL	2540	0.0217099	0.0484194	0	1.0685150
D2LINCAR	2824	0.0238082	0.0571442	0	1.2364571
D3LINCELL	1277	0.0348937	0.0767315	0	1.3578140
D3LINCAR	1449	0.0389857	0.0956528	0	1.6097272
		ENDUSE1=Q2			
TIME	8302	4.0446880	2.9425782	2.0000000	29.0000000
STRTRUE	9611	0.9997306	0.0335680	0.4791214	1.9318885
STRLINCELL	7293	0.9989305	0.0237255	0.6375966	1.3983686
STRLINCAR	8302	0.9983514	0.0278322	0.4697802	1.3178458
DIFLINCELL	7227	0.0072694	0.0278975	0	0.5683898
DIFLINCAR	7802	0.0076828	0.0326604	0	1.0989305
D2LINCELL	4641	0.0111990	0.0394394	0	1.1087869
D2LINCAR	5022	0.0113300	0.0531150	0	2.1978610
D3LINCELL	2098	0.0205221	0.0661589	0	0.9955389
D3LINCAR	2325	0.0191664	0.1007765	0	3.2967914
		ENDUSE1=Q3			

TIME	1259	4.1477363	3.0694817	2.0000000	28.0000000
STRTRUE	1451	1.0002257	0.0156591	0.7299592	1.1713918
STRLINCELL	1095	1.0000861	0.0119317	0.8648997	1.1093340
STRLINCAR	1259	1.0005957	0.0135063	0.8621825	1.1357410
DIFLINCELL	1086	0.0045118	0.0133264	0	0.1800272
DIFLINCAR	1187	0.0044735	0.0140487	0	0.1800272
D2LINCELL	693	0.0065031	0.0183865	0	0.3124069
D2LINCAR	756	0.0063107	0.0213526	0	0.3196945
D3LINCELL	336	0.0098889	0.0250145	0	0.2956747
D3LINCAR	381	0.0088134	0.0319202	0	0.3585526

ENDUSE1=Q4

TIME	2784	4.2018678	3.1797594	2.0000000	31.0000000
STRTRUE	3308	0.9999279	0.0257857	0.5832432	1.3617886
STRLINCELL	2449	0.9997496	0.0190100	0.7367702	1.1431452
STRLINCAR	2784	0.9998895	0.0202101	0.7367702	1.1538462
DIFLINCELL	2426	0.0065350	0.0232959	0	0.3319444
DIFLINCAR	2624	0.0066535	0.0256295	0	0.3691932
D2LINCELL	1563	0.0097633	0.0304870	0	0.4065187
D2LINCAR	1689	0.0096042	0.0361812	0	0.6745271
D3LINCELL	796	0.0144056	0.0449121	0	0.6097781
D3LINCAR	870	0.0121235	0.0574414	0	1.0117907

ENDUSE1=R0

TIME	1413	4.4331210	3.2681104	2.0000000	27.0000000
STRTRUE	1530	1.0043276	0.0932048	0.5430050	3.4000000
STRLINCELL	1138	0.9983861	0.0432805	0.5295090	1.2401961
STRLINCAR	1413	0.9977286	0.0491242	0.5252707	1.2661871
DIFLINCELL	1120	0.0258235	0.0466831	0	0.4166667
DIFLINCAR	1278	0.0296112	0.0711173	0	1.7333334
D2LINCELL	750	0.0324579	0.0596142	0	0.5786269
D2LINCAR	851	0.0369317	0.0804525	0	1.0666669
D3LINCELL	341	0.0424705	0.0809919	0	0.7065959
D3LINCAR	398	0.0496713	0.1078141	0	0.8571429

ENDUSE1=R1

TIME	3465	4.3012987	3.1228431	2.0000000	27.0000000
STRTRUE	3936	0.9983246	0.0483789	0.4320000	1.9191911
STRLINCELL	2892	0.9979957	0.0311842	0.7356322	1.3051775
STRLINCAR	3465	0.9953116	0.0344755	0.6048389	1.3051775
DIFLINCELL	2855	0.0176063	0.0339791	0	0.4704445
DIFLINCAR	3158	0.0188087	0.0372028	0	0.4704445
D2LINCELL	1785	0.0245673	0.0434339	0	0.5416667
D2LINCAR	1967	0.0273439	0.0533132	0	0.7159054
D3LINCELL	919	0.0347760	0.0593347	0	0.6302116
D3LINCAR	1013	0.0374826	0.0768643	0	0.6785502

ENDUSE1=R2

TIME	6562	4.0356599	2.8758717	2.0000000	33.0000000
STRTRUE	7733	0.9998644	0.0694854	0.2290744	6.0085437
STRLINCELL	5804	0.9975704	0.0332065	0.4766223	1.5384615
STRLINCAR	6562	0.9965249	0.0357833	0.4611679	1.5384615
DIFLINCELL	5761	0.0126234	0.0407360	0	0.9999149
DIFLINCAR	6215	0.0133425	0.0758595	0	5.0085520
D2LINCELL	3747	0.0199126	0.0703528	0	1.9998297
D2LINCAR	4036	0.0197693	0.0741107	0	2.3368150
D3LINCELL	1624	0.0316268	0.1110063	0	2.9997446
D3LINCAR	1792	0.0287046	0.1223993	0	3.5052224

ENDUSE1=R3

TIME	1812	3.8940397	2.7855087	2.0000000	26.0000000
STRTRUE	2131	0.9992863	0.0233400	0.7000000	1.2647777
STRLINCELL	1611	0.9990719	0.0198027	0.7004671	1.2124323
STRLINCAR	1812	0.9986925	0.0194168	0.7004459	1.2124323
DIFLINCELL	1588	0.0083366	0.0219669	0	0.4276187
DIFLINCAR	1701	0.0081362	0.0221404	0	0.4276620
D2LINCELL	992	0.0130412	0.0381810	0	0.8552374
D2LINCAR	1063	0.0125322	0.0387303	0	0.8553241
D3LINCELL	402	0.0226923	0.0484074	0	0.4370243
D3LINCAR	439	0.0196139	0.0517781	0	0.5074106

ENDUSE1=R4

TIME	5178	4.4333720	3.2020829	0	28.0000000
STRTRUE	6377	0.9994471	0.0322660	0.3449163	2.5000000
STRLINCELL	4427	0.9990551	0.0176688	0.5454545	1.1914829
STRLINCAR	5176	0.9982188	0.0198642	0.5454545	1.3375797
DIFLINCELL	4398	0.0072627	0.0319026	0	1.1431293
DIFLINCAR	4838	0.0075700	0.0321552	0	1.1444444
D2LINCELL	3058	0.0102021	0.0344374	0	0.8858801
D2LINCAR	3328	0.0103350	0.0346329	0	0.7888889
D3LINCELL	1507	0.0164676	0.0523135	0	1.3288201
D3LINCAR	1665	0.0160789	0.0489429	0	0.7571429

Appendix C: Order of programs:

1. Original data:

First run *inbls.sas*, which reads in the various ASCII datasets and creates SAS datasets.

Then run *merge.sas*, which creates *lib.itempr*

Then run *count.sas*, which creates IMPUTE1=1 within *lib.itempr*

Then run *variance.sas*, which creates IMPUTE1=2 within *lib.itempr*

2. Artificial data:

First run *artif.sas*, which creates *lib.artif*

Then run *acount.sas*, which creates IMPUTE1=1 within *lib.artifpr*

Then run *avarian.sas*, which creates IMPUTE1=2 within *lib.artifpr*

Run *actime.sas* to obtain histogram of time between non-imputed observations, for original and artificial data.

Then run *impute1.sas* to obtain results for carry forward and linear interpolation.

Run *impute2.sas* to obtain results for linear interpolation and hybrid of carry forward and linear interpolation.

3. Cell mean:

The program *impute3.sas* computes the value of the Laspeyres ratio indexes at the lower Enduse levels. It creates a new dataset *artifpr2.sd2,* which has the imputed values in the variable *ltrR*, and the true values in *ltr*.   Also need to run *impute3b.sas* until the dataset *temp.sd2* no longer increases in size.

Then run *impute4.sas* to obtain results hybrid technique and cell mean imputation.

4. Cell mean combined with linear:

Then run *impute5.sas* to obtain results from both hybrid techniques.

5. Cell mean by country of origin/destination:

Run *mergecon.sas*, which creates *lib.itemcon* and *lib.artifcon,* both of which include country of origin and exchange rate information.

The program *impute3.sas* computes the value of the Laspeyres ratio indexes at the lower Enduse levels. It creates a new dataset *artifpr2.sd2*, which has the imputed values in the variable *ltrR*, and the true values in *ltr*. Also need to run *impute3b.sas* until the dataset *temp.sd2* no longer increases in size.

Then run *imp4con.sas* to obtain results hybrid technique and cell mean imputation.

Then run *imp5con.sas* to obtain results from both hybrid techniques.